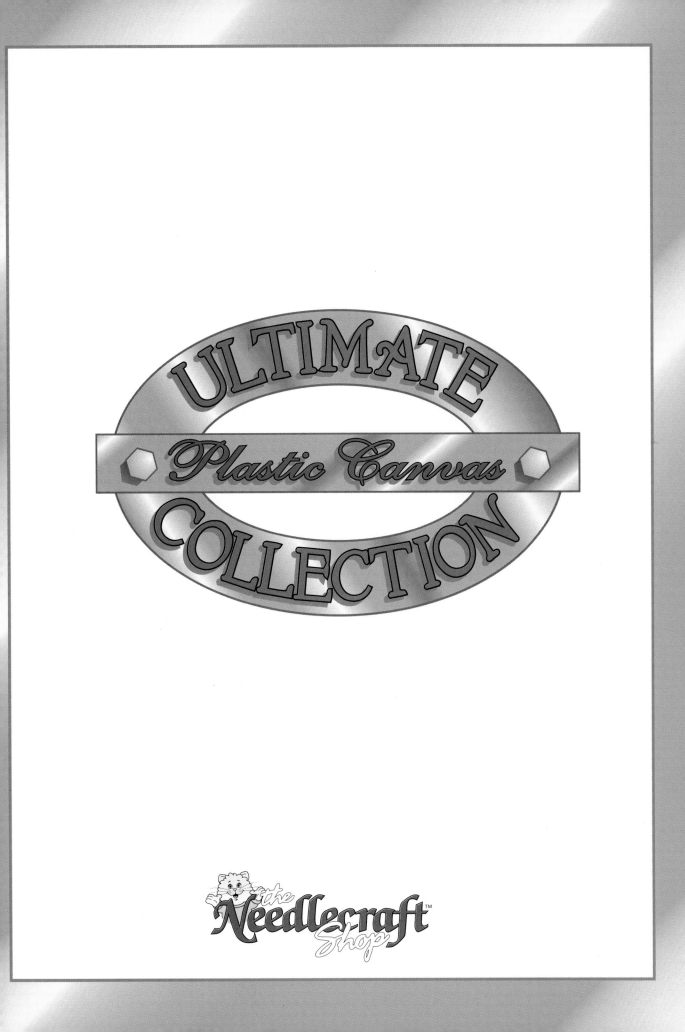

PUBLISHER / Donna Robertson
DESIGN DIRECTOR / Fran Rohus
PRODUCTION DIRECTOR / Ange Van Arman

EDITORIAL
Senior Editor / Janet Tipton
Editor / Kris Kirst
Assistant Graphics Editor / Glenda Chamberlain

PHOTOGRAPHY
Photographers / Russell Chaffin, Keith Godfrey
Photography Coordinator; Stylist / Ruth Whitaker
Assistant Photo Stylist / Jan Jaynes

PRODUCTION
Production & Layout / Debby Keel
Book Design / Diane Simpson
Color Specialist / Betty Radla

PRODUCT DESIGN
Design Coordinator / Pam Prather

BUSINESS
C.E.O. / John Robinson
Vice President / Marketing / Greg Deily
Vice President / M.I.S. / John Trotter

CREDITS
Sincerest thanks to all the designers, manufacturers and professionals
whose dedication has made this book possible.

Library of Congress Cataloging-in-Publication Data
ISBN: 1-57367-101-0
First Printing: 1998
Library of Congress Catalogue Number: 97-68260
Published and Distributed by *The Needlecraft Shop, LLC.,*
Big Sandy, Texas 75755
Printed in the United States of America

Dear Friends

I made some wonderful discoveries while exploring this *Ultimate* collection of plastic canvas needlework patterns. In addition to finding plenty of projects to keep me busy all year, I was also reminded of the many special friends I've made because of my passion for stitching. We share so many of the same creative impulses and satisfactions. Many of us find needlework to be the most effective, time-proven method of relaxation "therapy" – almost a meditative process that provides serenity as well as a sense of accomplishment.

Many of you have written to tell us about your charity work, about the ribbons you won at the county fair. You know that we, too, share a passion for stitchery that sometimes reaches beyond the comprehension of some of our otherwise-occupied friends and loved ones. But I do have a question for my fellow needlework enthusiasts – an issue hardly broached except by the most brutally honest among us. Do you get a little nervous, like I do, while putting the finishing touches on your latest project? You see, I'm the type who likes to have at least two more waiting-to-be-started projects at the ready. The prospect of not having some stitching in hand is just about more than I can bear.

This *Ultimate* collection will most definitely be added to my library shelves at home – a new source of never-ending ideas and a colorful rainbow of guaranteed tranquility.

Janet

Table of Contents

CHERISHED COUNTRY

SWEET SENSATIONS

FALL FRILLS

CHRISTMAS CHEER

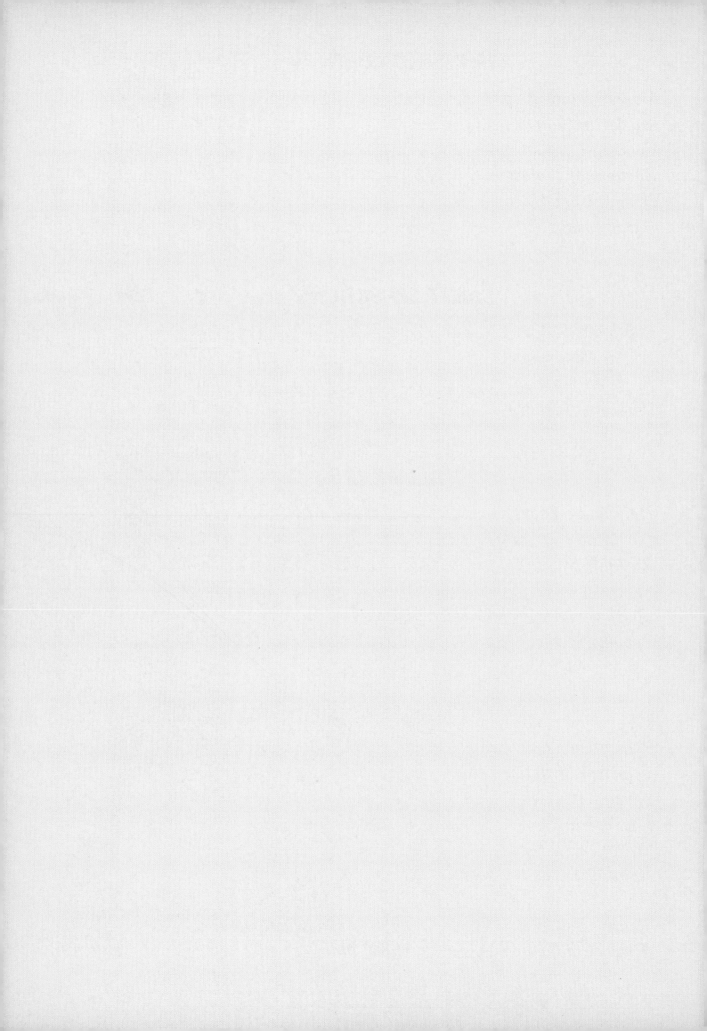

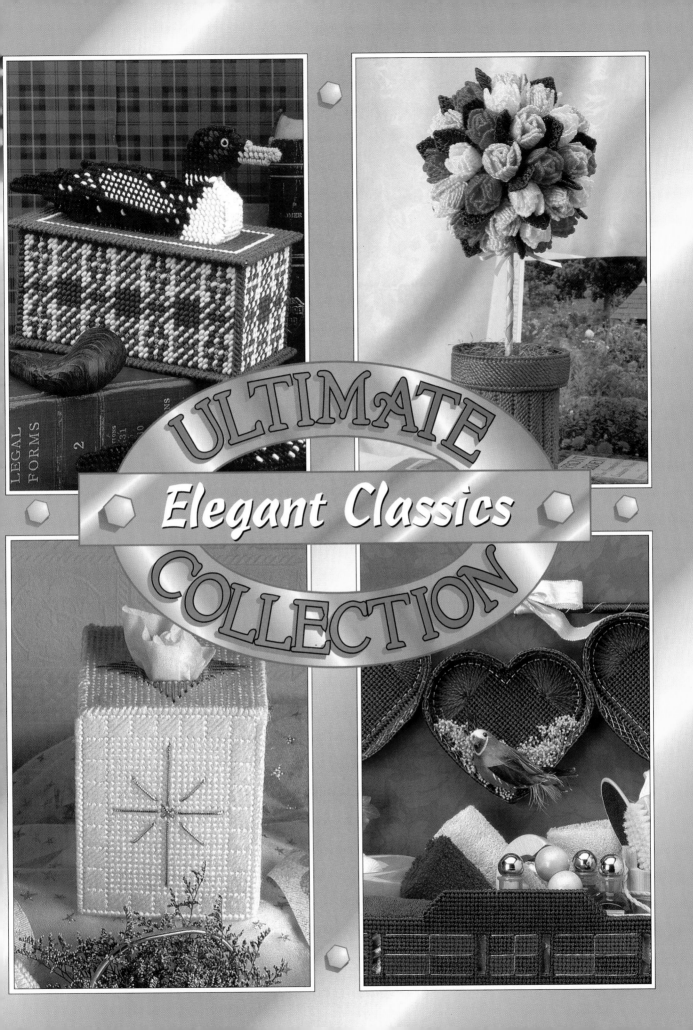

ULTIMATE COLLECTION

Elegant Classics

Topiary Tree

Designed by Carol Nartowicz

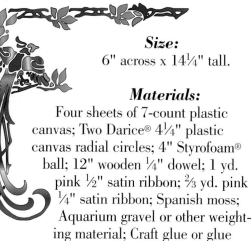

Size:
6" across x 14¼" tall.

Materials:
Four sheets of 7-count plastic canvas; Two Darice® 4¼" plastic canvas radial circles; 4" Styrofoam® ball; 12" wooden ¼" dowel; 1 yd. pink ½" satin ribbon; ⅔ yd. pink ¼" satin ribbon; Spanish moss; Aquarium gravel or other weighting material; Craft glue or glue gun; Worsted-weight or plastic canvas yarn; for amounts see Color Key.

Cutting Instructions:
A: For pot side, cut one 20 x 77 holes (no graph).

B: For pot rim, cut one 7 x 90 holes (no graph).

C: For pot rim bottom, cut one from one circle according to graph.

D: For pot bottom, cut away outer two rows of holes from remaining circle to measure 3½" across (no graph).

E: For rose petals, cut fifty-four according to graph.

F: For rose center pieces, cut one hundred sixty-two 2 x 7 holes (no graph).

G: For leaves, cut twenty-seven according to graph.

Stitching Instructions:
(Note: C and D pieces are not worked.)

1: Using colors and stitches indicated, work A (overlap two holes at short ends and work through both thicknesses at overlap area to join; pattern will not end evenly), E (work eighteen in each of the following colors: white, lt. pink and watermelon) and G pieces according to stitch pattern guide and graphs; with forest, Overcast edges of G pieces. Overlapping one hole at short ends and working through both thicknesses at overlap area to join, using dk. rust and Slanted Gobelin Stitch over narrow width, work B.

2: With dk. rust, Whipstitch and assemble A-D pieces, dowel and weight material as indicated on C graph and according to Pot Assembly Diagram.

3: With matching color, Whipstitch Y edges of

each E piece together; Overcast unfinished edges. For each rose center (make 18 in each rose color), Whipstitch three F pieces together according to Rose Center Assembly Diagram. For each rose (make 54), roll one E into a spiral around one matching-color rose center; glue or tack together to secure.

4: Insert opposite end of dowel 3" into foam ball; glue to secure, if desired. Glue a thin layer of Spanish moss around ball; glue flowers and leaves around ball as desired to cover (see photo).

5: Glue center of ¼" ribbon to dowel at edge of pot rim bottom, then wrap ends around dowel in a criss-cross pattern (see photo) and tie into bow under roses; glue bow to dowel to secure.

6: Glue Spanish moss inside pot to cover (see photo). ✧

C – Pot Rim Bottom
(cut 1)
Cut out gray area carefully.

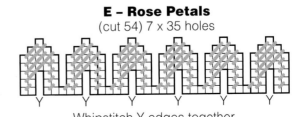

COLOR KEY: Topiary Tree

	Worsted-weight	Nylon Plus™	Need-loft®	YARN AMOUNT
☐	Lt. Pink	#10	#08	62 yds.
☐	White	#01	#41	62 yds.
☐	Watermelon	#54	#55	62 yds.
■	Forest	#32	#29	32 yds.
■	Dk. Rust	#16	#10	28 yds.
■	Flower Color			

STITCH KEY:
☐ Pot Side Attachment

Pot Assembly Diagram

Step 2: Glue one end of dowel to center of D.

Dowel

Overlap

Step 1: Whipstitch A and D pieces together.

Step 4: Whipstitch B and C pieces together; Overcast unfinished edges of B.

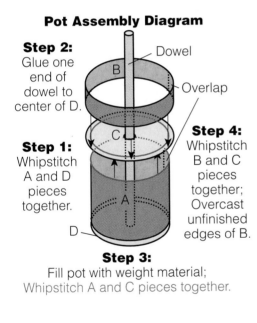

Step 3: Fill pot with weight material; Whipstitch A and C pieces together.

Rose Center Assembly Diagram

Step 1: For each rose center, Whipstitch three F pieces together.

F Assembly

Step 2: Run yarn lengthwise three times around each piece to cover; secure ends on wrong side.

Pot Side Stitch Pattern Guide

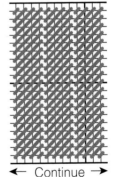

← Continue →
established pattern across length of entire piece.

G – Leaf
(cut 27)
7 x 9 holes

E – Rose Petals
(cut 54) 7 x 35 holes

Whipstitch Y edges together.

Decorate a den or study with majestic waterfowl when you create a doorstop, storage box and paperweight.

Loons Study Set

Designed by Darla J. Fanton

Size:
Doorstop is 6" x 15"; Paperweight is 3⅛" x 8½"; Storage Box is 6½" x 8¾".

Materials:
Two 12" x 18" or larger sheets of 7-count plastic canvas; Two 9-mm and four 6-mm yellow/black animal eyes (cut off shanks and file nubs smooth); One of each large (for Doorstop) and small (for Paperweight) zip-close bag filled with gravel or other weighting material; Craft glue or glue gun; ⅛" metallic ribbon or heavy metallic braid (for amount see Color Key on page 12); Worsted-weight or plastic canvas yarn (for amounts see Color Key).

Cutting Instructions:
(**Note:** Graphs on pages 12-14.)

A: For Doorstop sides, cut two according to graph.

B: For Doorstop breast, cut one according to graph.

C: For Doorstop base, cut one 11 x 45 holes (no graph).

D: For Doorstop tail, cut one according to graph.

E: For Doorstop wings, cut two according to graph.

F: For Paperweight/Storage Box sides, cut four (two for Paperweight and two for Storage Box) according to graph.

G: For Paperweight/Storage Box breast, cut two (one for Paperweight and one for Storage Box) according to graph.

H: For Paperweight/Storage Box tail, cut two (one for Paperweight and one for Storage Box) according to graph.

I: For Paperweight/Storage Box wings, cut four (two for Paperweight and two for Storage Box) according to graph.

J: For Paperweight base, cut one 8 x 27 holes.

K: For Storage Box sides, cut two 20 x 45 holes (no graph).

L: For Storage Box ends, cut two 20 x 20 holes (no graph).

M: For Storage Box base, cut one 24 x 48 holes.

N: For Storage Box lid top, cut one 24 x 48 holes.

O: For Storage Box lid sides, cut two 4 x 40 holes (no graph).

P: For Storage Box lid ends, cut two 4 x 16 holes (no graph).

Stitching Instructions:
(**Note:** C piece is not worked.)

1: Using colors and stitches indicated, work A, B, E-G and I-N (one A, one E, two F and two I pieces on opposite side of canvas) pieces according to graphs and stitch pattern guide; fill in uncoded areas and work D and H pieces using black and Continental Stitch; with black, Overcast edges of E and I pieces. Using eggshell and Continental Stitch, work O and P pieces.

2: Using black and Backstitch, embroider detail on E and I pieces as indicated on graphs.

3: For Doorstop, with matching colors, Whipstitch and assemble A-E pieces and large weight as indicated and according to Loon Assembly Diagram on page 13.

4: For Paperweight, with matching colors, Whipstitch two F, one G, one H, two I, J and small weight as indicated and according to Loon Assembly Diagram.

5: For Storage Box, omitting weight and base, Whipstitch remaining F-H pieces together as indicated and according to Loon Assembly Diagram; Whipstitch assembly and K-P pieces together as indicated and according to Storage Box & Lid Assembly Diagram on page 14.

6: Glue one large eye to each A piece and one small eye to each F piece as indicated.✧

Loons Study Set
Photo on page 10

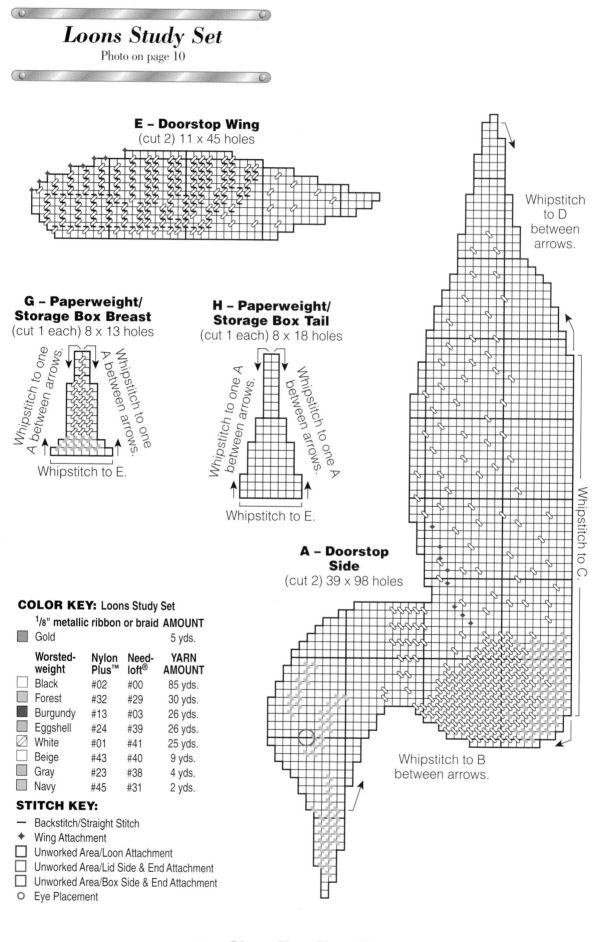

E – Doorstop Wing
(cut 2) 11 x 45 holes

G – Paperweight/
Storage Box Breast
(cut 1 each) 8 x 13 holes

Whipstitch to one A between arrows.

Whipstitch to one A between arrows.

Whipstitch to E.

H – Paperweight/
Storage Box Tail
(cut 1 each) 8 x 18 holes

Whipstitch to one A between arrows.

Whipstitch to one A between arrows.

Whipstitch to E.

A – Doorstop
Side
(cut 2) 39 x 98 holes

Whipstitch to D between arrows.

Whipstitch to C.

Whipstitch to B between arrows.

COLOR KEY: Loons Study Set

1/8" metallic ribbon or braid			AMOUNT
Gold			5 yds.

Worsted-weight	Nylon Plus™	Need-loft®	YARN AMOUNT
Black	#02	#00	85 yds.
Forest	#32	#29	30 yds.
Burgundy	#13	#03	26 yds.
Eggshell	#24	#39	26 yds.
White	#01	#41	25 yds.
Beige	#43	#40	9 yds.
Gray	#23	#38	4 yds.
Navy	#45	#31	2 yds.

STITCH KEY:
— Backstitch/Straight Stitch
✦ Wing Attachment
☐ Unworked Area/Loon Attachment
☐ Unworked Area/Lid Side & End Attachment
☐ Unworked Area/Box Side & End Attachment
○ Eye Placement

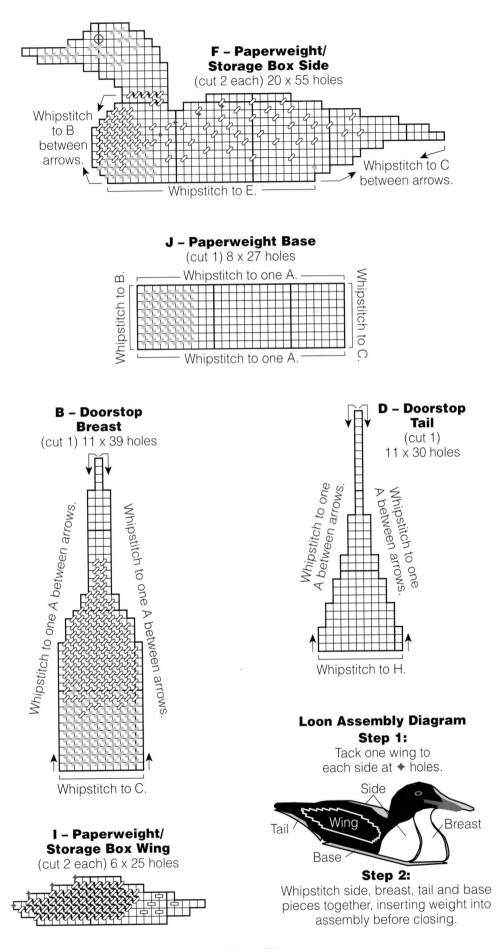

F – Paperweight/ Storage Box Side

(cut 2 each) 20 x 55 holes

Whipstitch to B between arrows.

Whipstitch to E.

Whipstitch to C between arrows.

J – Paperweight Base

(cut 1) 8 x 27 holes

Whipstitch to B.

Whipstitch to one A.

Whipstitch to one A.

Whipstitch to C.

B – Doorstop Breast

(cut 1) 11 x 39 holes

Whipstitch to one A between arrows.

Whipstitch to one A between arrows.

Whipstitch to C.

D – Doorstop Tail

(cut 1)
11 x 30 holes

Whipstitch to one A between arrows.

Whipstitch to one A between arrows.

Whipstitch to H.

Loon Assembly Diagram
Step 1:
Tack one wing to each side at ✦ holes.

Side

Wing

Tail

Breast

Base

Step 2:
Whipstitch side, breast, tail and base pieces together, inserting weight into assembly before closing.

I – Paperweight/ Storage Box Wing

(cut 2 each) 6 x 25 holes

Loons Study Set

Photo on page 10

M – Storage Box Base (cut 1) 24 x 48 holes

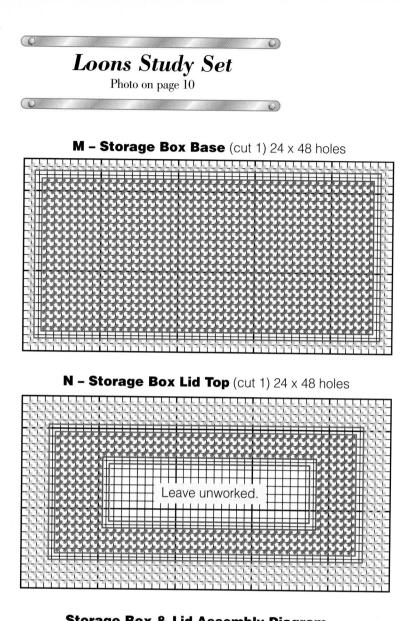

N – Storage Box Lid Top (cut 1) 24 x 48 holes

Leave unworked.

Storage Box Side & End Stitch Pattern Guide

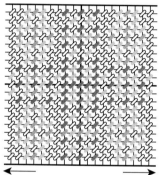

Continue established pattern across each entire piece.

Storage Box & Lid Assembly Diagram

Step 1:
With matching colors, Whipstitch loon assembly to indicated area on right side of N.

Loon Assembly

N

Step 2:
With eggshell, Whipstitch O and P pieces together and to indicated area on wrong side of N; with matching colors, Overcast edges of lid sides and lid.

O   P
P   O

Step 3:
With forest, Whipstitch K and L pieces together and to unworked area on right side of M; Overcast edges of box sides and base.

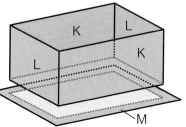

K   L
L   K

M

COLOR KEY: Loons Study Set

1/8" metallic ribbon or braid			AMOUNT
Gold			5 yds.

Worsted-weight	Nylon Plus™	Need-loft®	YARN AMOUNT
Black	#02	#00	85 yds.
Forest	#32	#29	30 yds.
Burgundy	#13	#03	26 yds.
Eggshell	#24	#39	26 yds.
White	#01	#41	25 yds.
Beige	#43	#40	9 yds.
Gray	#23	#38	4 yds.
Navy	#45	#31	2 yds.

STITCH KEY:

— Backstitch/Straight Stitch

✦ Wing Attachment

☐ Unworked Area/Loon Attachment

☐ Unworked Area/Lid Side & End Attachment

☐ Unworked Area/Box Side & End Attachment

○ Eye Placement

Forget-me-not Bureau Scarf

Designed by Michele Wilcox

Size:
12" x 17".

Materials:
One 12" x 18" or larger sheet of 7-count plastic canvas; Worsted-weight or plastic canvas yarn (for amounts see Color Key on page 24.)

Cutting Instructions:
A: For Scarf, cut one according to graph on page 24.

Stitching Instructions:
1: Using colors and stitches indicated, work piece according to graph. With matching colors, Overcast edges.✧

*Add elegant sparkle
to your private chambers
with a trio of
smart accents.*

Winter Jewels

Designed by Betty Radla

Size:
Tissue Cover snugly covers a boutique-style tissue box; Box is 6⅛" square x 3" tall; Mirror Frame is 7⅛" x 12¾", with a 3½" x 9¼" mirror opening.

Materials:
Five sheets of 7-count plastic canvas; 6¼" x 12" mirror; Metallic cord (for amount see Color Key on page 18); Worsted-weight or plastic canvas yarn (for amount see Color Key).

Cutting Instructions:
(**Note:** Graphs on pages 18 & 19.)

A: For Tissue Cover top, cut one according to graph.

B: For Tissue Cover sides, cut four 29 x 37 holes.

C: For Box lid top, cut one 39 x 39 holes.

D: For Box lid sides, cut four 3 x 39 holes (no graph).

E: For Box sides, cut four 18 x 37 holes (no graph).

F: For Box bottom, cut one 37 x 37 holes (no graph).

G: For Mirror Frame front, cut one according to graph.

H: For Mirror Frame back, cut one 46 x 84 holes (no graph).

Stitching Instructions:
(**Note:** F and H pieces are not worked.)

1: Using white and stitches indicated, work B, C, E and G pieces according to graphs and stitch pattern guide. Fill in uncoded areas of B and C pieces and work A using white and Continental Stitch; fill in uncoded areas of G using white and Reverse Continental Stitch. Using white and Slanted Gobelin Stitch over narrow width, work D pieces.

2: Using gold and embroidery stitches indicated, embroider A-C and G pieces as indicated on graphs. With matching colors as shown in photo, Overcast cutout edges of A and G pieces.

3: For Tissue Cover, with white, Whipstitch A and B pieces together, forming Cover; Overcast unfinished bottom edges.

4: With white, Whipstitch C and D pieces together, forming lid, and E and F pieces together, forming box; Overcast unfinished edges of box and lid.

5: For Mirror Frame, holding H to wrong side of G with mirror between, with white, Whipstitch together. ✧

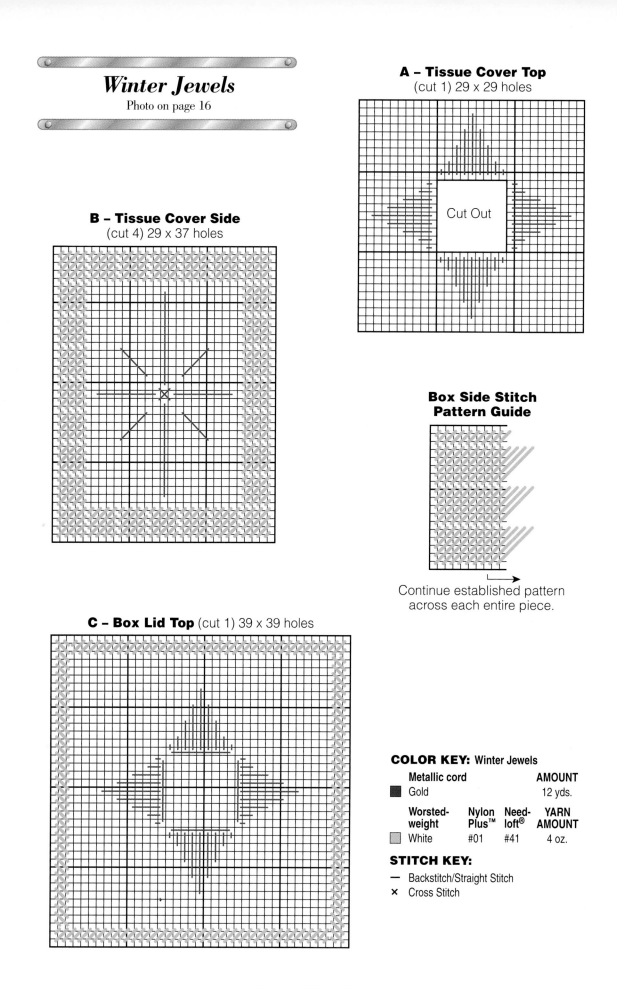

Winter Jewels

Photo on page 16

A – Tissue Cover Top
(cut 1) 29 x 29 holes

Cut Out

B – Tissue Cover Side
(cut 4) 29 x 37 holes

Box Side Stitch Pattern Guide

Continue established pattern
across each entire piece.

C – Box Lid Top (cut 1) 39 x 39 holes

COLOR KEY: Winter Jewels

			AMOUNT
Metallic cord			
Gold			12 yds.

Worsted-weight	Nylon Plus™	Need-loft®	YARN AMOUNT
White	#01	#41	4 oz.

STITCH KEY:

— Backstitch/Straight Stitch
× Cross Stitch

G – Mirror Frame Front (cut 1) 46 x 84 holes

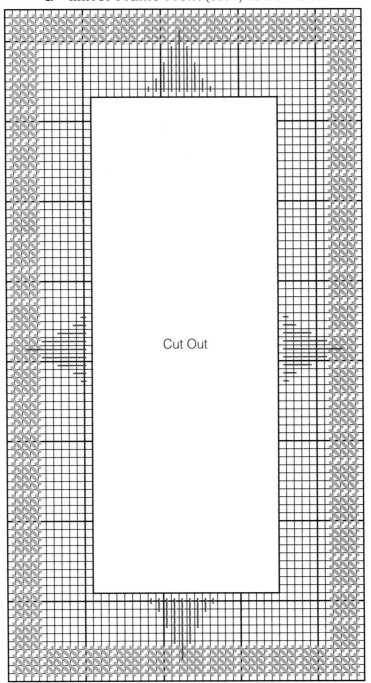

Cut Out

Shimmering Bath Ensemble

Designed by Betty Radla

Size:
Tray is 7¼" x 18¼" x 3⅞" tall; Wall Hanging is 1¼" x 7¾" x 19¼" across, not including embellishments.

Materials:
Two sheets of 12" x 18" or larger 7- count plastic canvas; Three Uniek® Crafts 6" plastic canvas heart shapes; 17" wooden ¼" dowel; Artificial bird; Small amount of baby's breath; 1 yd. metallic gold 1" mesh ribbon; 16" x 24" piece of metallic gold fabric; Sewing needle and metallic gold thread; Craft glue or glue gun; Fine metallic braid or metallic thread (for amount see Color Key on page 22); Worsted-weight or plastic canvas yarn (for amounts see Color Key).

Cutting Instructions:

(**Note:** Graphs on pages 22 & 23.)

A: For Tray sides and linings, cut four (two for sides and two for linings) according to graph.

B: For Tray ends and linings, cut four (two for ends and two for linings) according to graph.

C: For Tray bottom, cut one 47 x 120 holes (no graph).

D: For Wall Hanging heart backs, use heart shapes.

E: For Wall Hanging heart side pieces, cut six 7 x 64 holes (no graph).

Stitching Instructions:

(**Note:** Lining A, lining B and C pieces are not worked.)

1: Using colors and stitches indicated, work two A, two B and D pieces according to graphs; fill in uncoded areas and work E pieces using navy and Continental Stitch. With navy, Overcast cutout edges of A and B pieces.

2: Using metallic braid or thread and Straight Stitch, embroider detail on A, B and D pieces as indicated on graphs.

3: With navy, Whipstitch and assemble A-C pieces and fabric according to Tray Assembly Diagram.

4: For each heart (make 3), with navy, Whipstitch one D and two E pieces together according to Heart Assembly Diagram on page 23; Overcast unfinished edges.

5: Using metallic braid or thread, embroider detail around sides of each heart assembly according to Chain Link Stitch Pattern Guide on page 22.

6: Placing a small amount of glue on dowel ahead as you wrap and securing ends under wraps, wrap dowel with navy yarn to cover, then wrap metallic braid or thread over navy to embellish (see photo). Glue hearts to dowel as shown in photo; glue bird and baby's breath inside center heart as shown. Wrap ribbon around center of dowel and tie ends into a bow.

7: Hang as desired.✧

Tray Assembly Diagram

Step 1:
Holding lining A and B pieces to wrong side of matching worked pieces, Whipstitch to C through all thicknesses.

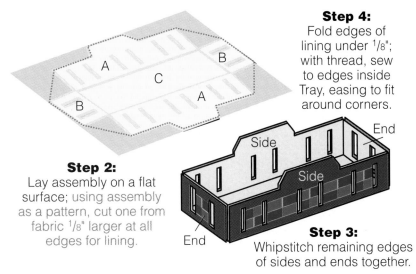

Step 4:
Fold edges of lining under ¹/₈"; with thread, sew to edges inside Tray, easing to fit around corners.

Step 2:
Lay assembly on a flat surface; using assembly as a pattern, cut one from fabric ¹/₈" larger at all edges for lining.

Step 3:
Whipstitch remaining edges of sides and ends together.

Shimmering Bath Ensemble

Photo on page 20

COLOR KEY: Shimmering Bath

Fine metallic braid or thread			AMOUNT
■ Gold			38 yds.

Worsted-weight	Nylon Plus™	Need-loft®	YARN AMOUNT
■ Navy	#45	#31	3 oz.
■ Burgundy	#13	#03	30 yds.
■ Forest	#32	#29	30 yds.

STITCH KEY:

— Backstitch/Straight Stitch

Chain Link Stitch Pattern Guide

(Background stitches not shown for clarity; embroidery stitches shown in different colors for contrast.)

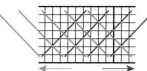

Continue established pattern over seams and around each side piece.
(**NOTE:** Work all purple stitches first.)

A – Tray Side & Lining
(cut 2 each)
24 x 120 holes

B – Tray End & Lining
(cut 2 each) 17 x 47 holes

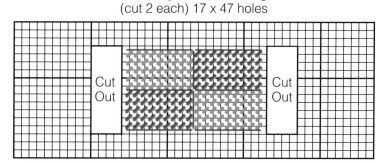

Heart Assembly Diagram

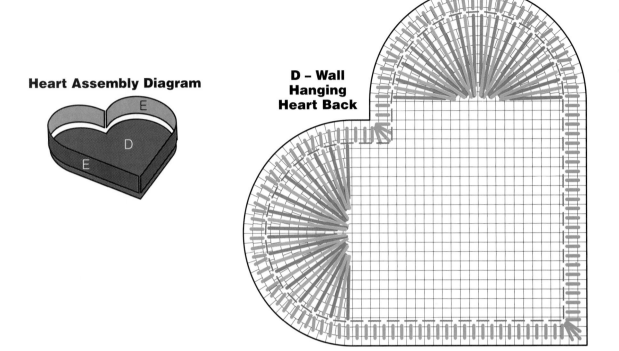

D – Wall Hanging Heart Back

Forget-me-not Bureau Scarf

Photo on page 15

A – Scarf (cut 1) 80 x 113 holes
Cut out gray areas carefully.

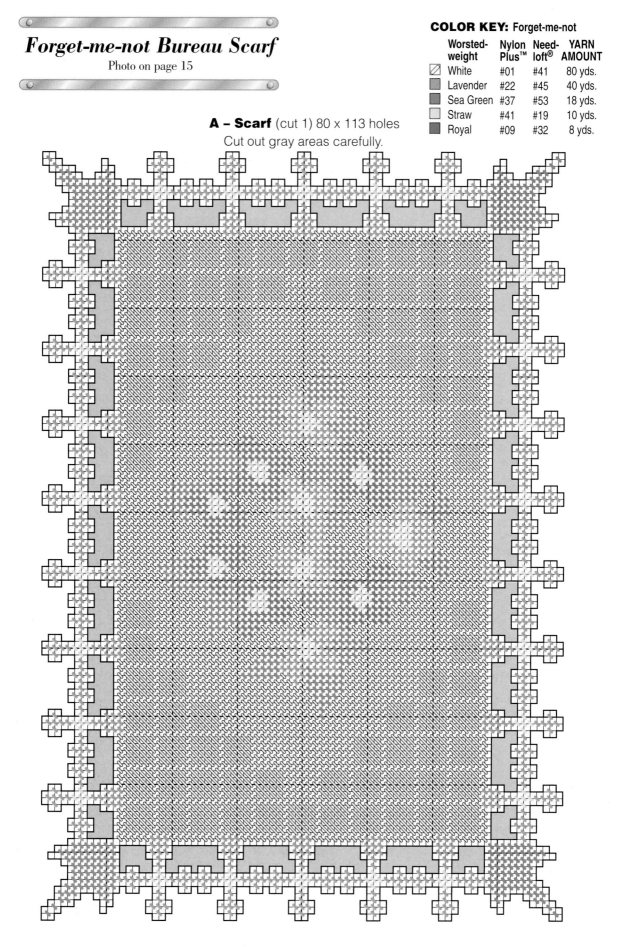

Blessed are the pure in heart,
For they will see God.
— Matthew 5:8

ULTIMATE

Loving Inspirations

COLLECTION

HOLY BIBLE

The path through
life may often
roam,
yet it's here
my heart feels
most at home

Blessed are the pure in heart,
For they will see God.

—— MATTHEW 5:8

Create a loving memorial or devotional focal point in your private sanctuary.

Daily Inspirations

Designed by Diane T. Ray

Size:
11½" x 16¼",
with a 4½" x 5"
photo window.

Materials:
Two sheets of 12" x 18" or
larger sheets of 7-count plastic
canvas; Two Uniek® Crafts 6"
plastic canvas heart shapes; 1 yd.
white ¾" lace edging; Artificial leaves
and pink/white baby's breath flowers; One 7" x
7" piece of clear plastic (optional); Craft glue or
glue gun; Metallic cord (for amounts see Color
Key); Worsted-weight or plastic canvas yarn (for
amounts see Color Key).

Cutting Instructions:

A: For cross front and backing, cut two (one for
front and one for backing) according to
graph.

B: For heart frame front, cut one from one
heart shape according to graph.

C: For heart frame backing, use
remaining heart shape (no graph).

D: For optional photo window protector,
using C as a pattern, cut one from
clear plastic according to graph ⅛"
smaller at all edges.

Stitching Instructions:
(**Note:** Backing A and C pieces are not
worked.)

1: Using colors and stitches indicated, work
one A for front and B pieces according to
graphs. With white/silver cord, Overcast
cutout edges of B.

2: Using black (separate into plies, if desired)
and embroidery stitches indicated, embroider detail on front A as indicated on graph.

3: Holding backing A to wrong side of front,
with matching colors, Whipstitch together.
Holding C to wrong side of B, with lavender,
Whipstitch together as indicated; Overcast
unfinished edges.

4: Create message, and trim to fit inside frame;
slide message and D (if desired) into frame.

5: Glue lace to back of frame around outer
edges (see photo), trimming away excess as
needed to fit. Glue frame to cross; glue flowers and leaves to frame as desired or as
shown in photo.

6: Hang as desired.✧

COLOR KEY: Daily Inspirations

Metallic cord			AMOUNT
White/Silver			9 yds.
Silver			4 yds.

Worsted-weight	Nylon Plus™	Needloft®	YARN AMOUNT
White	#01	#41	18 yds.
Purple	#21	#46	15 yds.
Lavender	#22	#45	6 yds.
Black	#02	#00	1 yd.

STITCH KEY:
— Backstitch/Straight Stitch

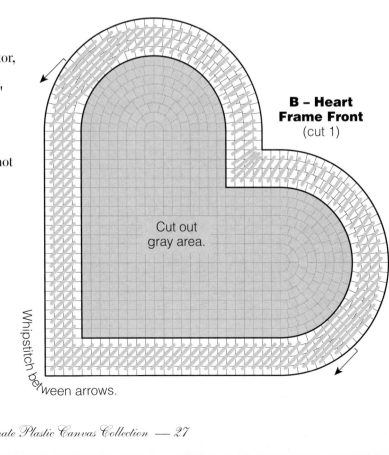

**B – Heart
Frame Front**
(cut 1)

Cut out
gray area.

Whipstitch between arrows.

A – Cross Front & Backing
(cut 1 each)
75 x 107 holes

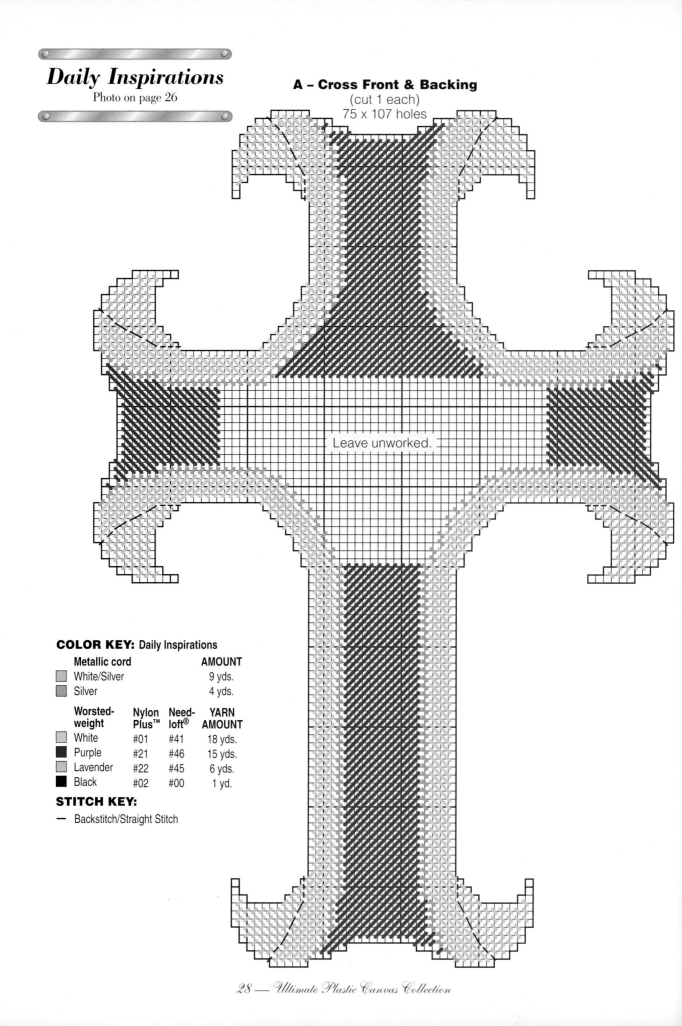

Leave unworked.

COLOR KEY: Daily Inspirations

Metallic cord			AMOUNT
White/Silver			9 yds.
Silver			4 yds.

Worsted-weight	Nylon Plus™	Need-loft®	YARN AMOUNT
White	#01	#41	18 yds.
Purple	#21	#46	15 yds.
Lavender	#22	#45	6 yds.
Black	#02	#00	1 yd.

STITCH KEY:

— Backstitch/Straight Stitch

The Nativity

Designed by Dianne Davis

Instructions on page 30

Bring to life the blessed birth when you recreate the Nativity using porcelain doll parts, shimmering metallics and lustrous pearl cotton stitched on 10-count canvas.

The Nativity

Photo on page 29

Size:

Mary and Joseph each are 6" across x 10" tall; Baby Jesus is 1" x 3¼" x 4"; Manger is 2½" x 4" x 5", including legs.

Materials:

Four sheets of 10-count plastic canvas; One set each of porcelain doll parts: Mary doll head with hands, Joseph doll head with hands and Baby Jesus doll head with hands; 16" of ¼" x ½" balsa wood; Sharp woodworking or utility knife; Dk. brown acrylic paint; Small paintbrush; ¼ yd. silver ⅛" metallic ribbon; Spanish moss; Monofilament fishing line; Craft glue or glue gun; Kreinik heavy (#32) metallic braid (for amounts see Color Key); #3 pearl cotton or six-strand embroidery floss (for amounts see Color Key).

Cutting Instructions:

(**Note:** Graphs continued on pages 42-48.)

A: For Mary's cape, cut one according to graph.

B: For Mary's dress insert, cut one according to graph.

C: For Mary's sleeve fronts #1 and #2, cut one each according to graphs.

D: For Mary's sleeve backs #1 and #2, cut one each according to graphs.

E: For Joseph's cape, cut one according to graph.

F: For Joseph's cape insert, cut one according to graph.

G: For Joseph's sleeve fronts #1 and #2, cut one each according to graphs.

H: For Joseph's sleeve backs #1 and #2, cut one each according to graphs.

I: For Baby Jesus' blanket, cut one according to graph.

J: For Manger sides, cut two 16 x 43 holes (no graph).

K: For Manger ends, cut two according to graph.

L: For Manger bottom, cut one 11 x 43 holes (no graph).

M: For Manger legs, cut four from balsa wood according to Manger Leg Cutting Guide.

Stitching Instructions:

(**Note:** Use #3 pearl cotton or six strands floss throughout.)

1: Using colors and stitches indicated and leaving uncoded tab areas of C and G pieces unworked, work A-E and G-L pieces according to graphs and stitch pattern guide. Using rose and Continental Stitch, work F. With white for Mary's dress insert and cutout edges of blanket, silver for trim edges of Mary's cape as indicated on graph, tan for Joseph's cape and with matching colors, Overcast edges of A, B, E and F pieces and cutout edges of I.

2: For each sleeve, holding corresponding sleeve front and back wrong sides together, with matching color, Whipstitch together as indicated; omitting tabs, with silver for cuff edges of Mary's sleeves as indicated and with matching colors, Overcast unfinished edges of sleeves.

3: For Mary, glue A and B pieces together according to Cape Assembly Diagram on page 45. Insert tab of each sleeve through corresponding cutout on cape; glue tab to inside of cape to secure. (**Note:** Do not glue sleeve to front of cape.) Insert head up from bottom through top of assembly; to secure head, with fishing line, sew through cape under "shoulder" edges to hold head up. Insert hands through cuff openings (see photo) and glue to cape; glue sleeve to cape over hands to secure.

4: For Joseph, substituting Joseph pieces for Mary pieces, follow Step 3.

5: Tie silver ⅛" metallic ribbon into a bow and glue to top edges of Mary's cape as shown.

6: With white, Whipstitch I together as indicated and according to Blanket Assembly Diagram on page 48. Insert Jesus' arms through cutouts on blanket and glue to blanket to secure.

(**Note:** Paint M pieces; let dry.)

7: Whipstitch and assemble J-M pieces as indicated and according to Manger Assembly Diagram on page 48.

8: Fill Manger with moss; place Baby Jesus in Manger.✧

M – Manger Leg Cutting Guide

(top view)

4"

1/2"

Notch   Balsa Wood

1"   2"

(side view)
Cut notch to half thickness of wood.

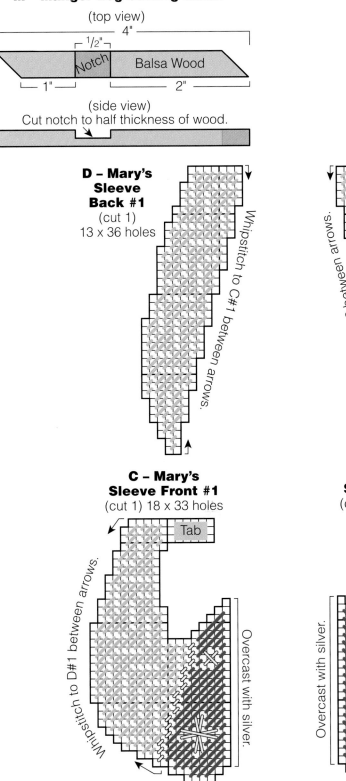

D – Mary's Sleeve Back #1
(cut 1)
13 x 36 holes

Whipstitch to C#1 between arrows.

D – Mary's Sleeve Back #2
(cut 1)
13 x 36 holes

Whipstitch to C#2 between arrows.

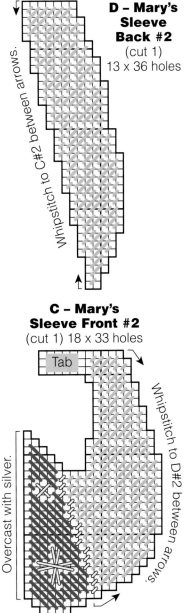

C – Mary's Sleeve Front #1
(cut 1) 18 x 33 holes

Tab

Whipstitch to D#1 between arrows.

Overcast with silver.

C – Mary's Sleeve Front #2
(cut 1) 18 x 33 holes

Tab

Overcast with silver.

Whipstitch to D#2 between arrows.

Lacy Coverlet

**Designed by Sandra Miller Maxfield
and Jimmy & Jessie Lampin**

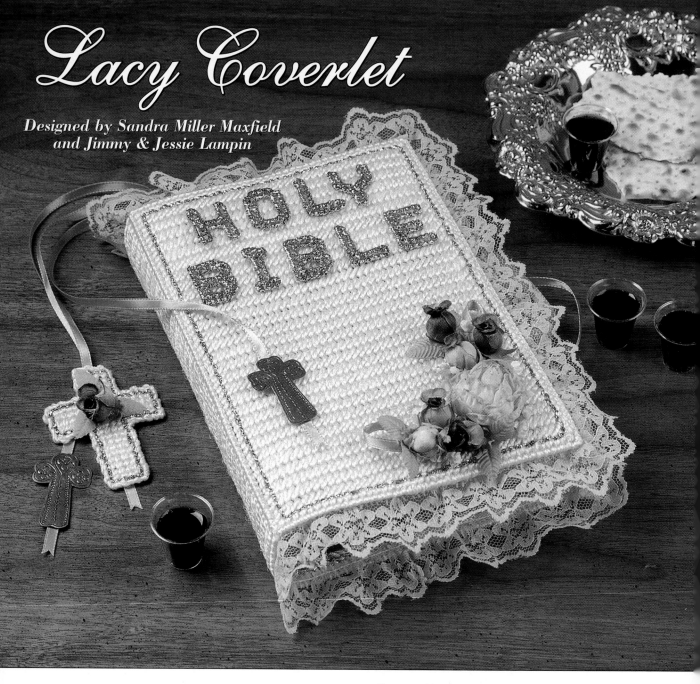

Size:
Fits a 1¼" x 5½" x 8½" Bible.

Materials:
Two sheets of 7-count plastic canvas; Assorted blue rosebuds with leaves and small flowers; Two metal 1½" x 2" crosses or symbols of choice; 2 yds. peach ¼" satin ribbon; 1½ yds. peach 1¼" pre-gathered lace; Craft glue or glue gun; Metallic cord (for amount see Color Key); Worsted-weight or plastic canvas yarn (for amount see Color Key).

Cutting Instructions:
A: For front and back, cut two (one for front and one for back) 42 x 61 holes (no graph).

B: For spine, cut one 10 x 61 holes (no graph).

C: For inner flaps, cut two 24 x 61 holes (no graph).

D: For cross, cut one according to graph.

E: For letters, cut number indicated according to graphs.

Stitching Instructions:
(**Note:** C pieces are not worked.)

1: Using eggshell and stitches indicated, work A, B and D pieces according to graph and stitch pattern guides; with cord for letters and eggshell for cross, Overcast edges of D and E pieces.

2: Using cord and Backstitch, embroider detail on A and B pieces as indicated on Front & Back Stitch Pattern Guide and on D piece as indicated on graph.

3: For Cover, with eggshell, Whipstitch A-C pieces together according to Bible Cover Assembly Diagram; Overcast unfinished edges.
(**Note:** Cut two 6½" and three 15" lengths of ribbon.)

4: Glue lace around inner edge of Cover as shown in photo. For bookmarks, glue one end of each 15" ribbon to inside of Cover at top edge of spine (see photo); trim ends as desired. Glue cross or other symbols and D to opposite end of ribbons as shown. For each handle, glue ends of one 6½" ribbon to inside of Cover at outer side edge.

5: Cut remaining ribbon in half; fold each ribbon in half and glue ends together. Adorn Cover and cross with ribbon, rosebuds, leaves and flowers as desired or as shown.✧

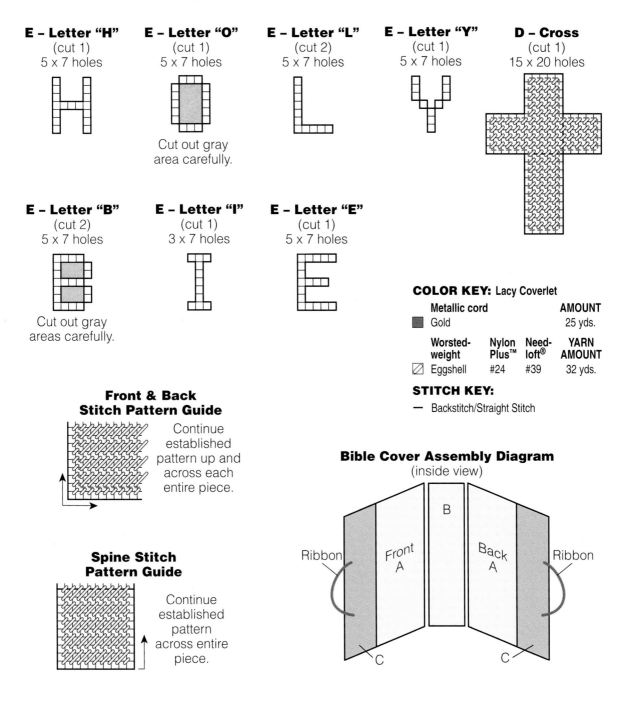

E – Letter "H"
(cut 1)
5 x 7 holes

E – Letter "O"
(cut 1)
5 x 7 holes

Cut out gray area carefully.

E – Letter "L"
(cut 2)
5 x 7 holes

E – Letter "Y"
(cut 1)
5 x 7 holes

D – Cross
(cut 1)
15 x 20 holes

E – Letter "B"
(cut 2)
5 x 7 holes

Cut out gray areas carefully.

E – Letter "I"
(cut 1)
3 x 7 holes

E – Letter "E"
(cut 1)
5 x 7 holes

COLOR KEY: Lacy Coverlet

Metallic cord			AMOUNT
▓ Gold			25 yds.

Worsted-weight	Nylon Plus™	Need-loft®	YARN AMOUNT
▨ Eggshell	#24	#39	32 yds.

STITCH KEY:
— Backstitch/Straight Stitch

Front & Back Stitch Pattern Guide

Continue established pattern up and across each entire piece.

Spine Stitch Pattern Guide

Continue established pattern across entire piece.

Bible Cover Assembly Diagram
(inside view)

Ribbon   Front A   B   Back A   Ribbon

C   C

House Blessing

Designed by Michele Wilcox

Size:
7⅝" x 10¾",
not including ruffle.

Materials:
One sheet of 7-count plastic
canvas; 2 yds. off-white 1¾"
eyelet ruffle; Craft glue or glue
gun; Worsted-weight or plastic canvas
yarn (for amounts see Color Key).

COLOR KEY: House Blessing

	Worsted-weight	Nylon Plus™	Need-loft®	YARN AMOUNT
☐	Eggshell	#24	#39	43 yds.
◻	Dusty Blue	#38	#34	13 yds.
◻	Dusty Rose	#52	#06	10 yds.
◻	Burgundy	#13	#03	6 yds.
◻	Mint	#30	#24	5 yds.
◼	Black	#02	#00	2 yds.

Cutting Instructions:
A: For sampler, cut one 50 x 70
holes.

Stitching Instructions:
1: Using colors and stitches indicated, work sampler according to
graph; with eggshell, Overcast
edges.

2: Glue ruffle to back of sampler
around outer edges (see photo),
trimming away excess as needed
to fit.

3: Hang as desired. ✧

A – Sampler
(cut 1) 50 x 70 holes

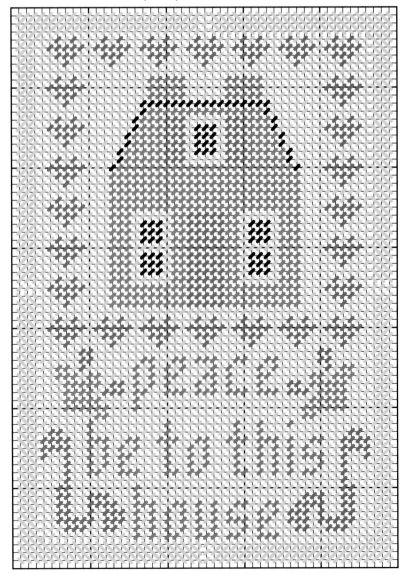

Guardian Angel

Designed by Jacquelyn Fox

Size:
10⅝" x 12¼".

Materials:
Two sheets of 7-count plastic canvas; Craft glue or glue gun; Worsted-weight or plastic canvas yarn (for amounts see Color Key).

Cutting Instructions:
(**Note:** Graphs continued on page 38.)
A: For heart, cut one according to graph.
B: For wings, cut one according to graph.
C: For head, cut one according to graph.

D: For hand #1 and #2, cut one each according to graphs.

Stitching Instructions:
1: Using dk. red and Continental Stitch, work A; using colors and stitches indicated (leave ¼" loops on Rya Knot stitches), work B-D pieces according to graphs. With royal for wings and with matching colors, Overcast edges of A-D pieces.
2: Using black (separate into plies, if desired) and embroidery stitches indicated, embroider detail on A, C and D pieces as indicated on graphs.
3: Glue head to front of wings; glue wings to back and hands to front of heart (see photo). Hang as desired. ✧

COLOR KEY: Guardian Angel

	Worsted-weight	Nylon Plus™	Need-loft®	YARN AMOUNT
■	Dk. Red	#20	#01	60 yds.
■	White	#01	#41	39 yds.
□	Sail Blue	#04	#35	20 yds.
■	Royal	#09	#32	19 yds.
▨	Straw	#41	#19	18 yds.
□	Flesh	#14	#56	16 yds.
■	Pink	#11	#07	2 yds.
■	Black	#02	#00	1 yd.

STITCH KEY:
— Backstitch/Straight Stitch
∽ Rya Knot

C – Head
(cut 1) 24 x 31 holes

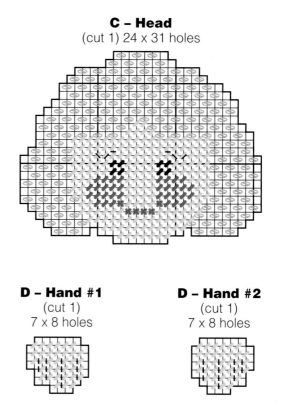

D – Hand #1
(cut 1)
7 x 8 holes

D – Hand #2
(cut 1)
7 x 8 holes

Guardian Angel

Photo on page 37

COLOR KEY: Guardian Angel

	Worsted-weight	Nylon Plus™	Need-loft®	YARN AMOUNT
Dk. Red	#20	#01	60 yds.
White	#01	#41	39 yds.
Sail Blue	#04	#35	20 yds.
Royal	#09	#32	19 yds.
Straw	#41	#19	18 yds.
Flesh	#14	#56	16 yds.
Pink	#11	#07	2 yds.
Black	#02	#00	1 yd.

STITCH KEY:

— Backstitch/Straight Stitch

↶ Rya Knot

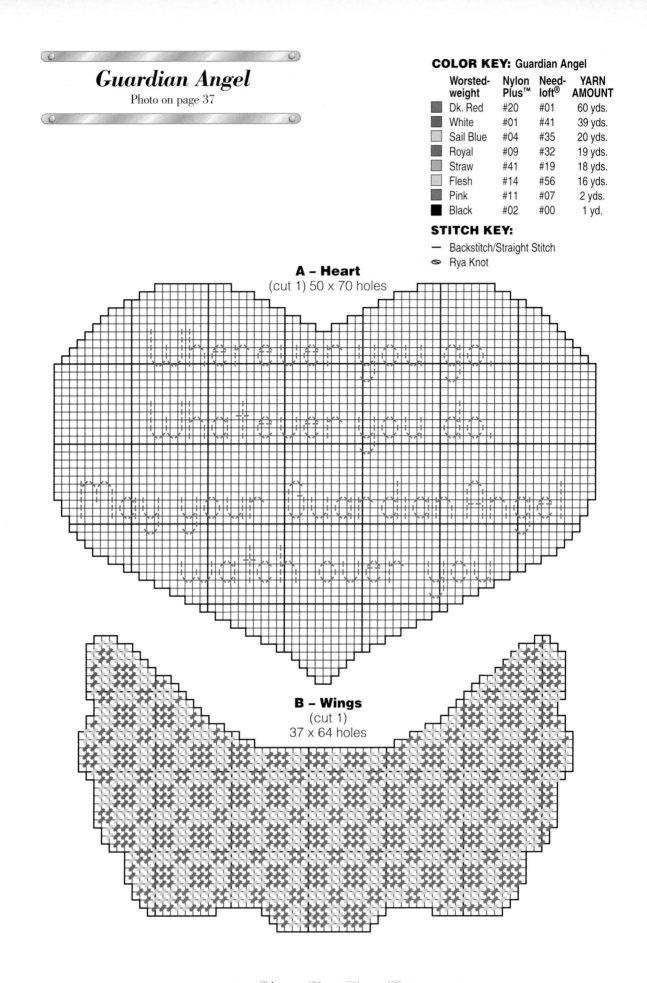

A – Heart
(cut 1) 50 x 70 holes

B – Wings
(cut 1)
37 x 64 holes

Path Through Life

Designed by Jacquelyn Fox

Instructions on page 40

The path through life may often roam, yet it's here my heart feels most at home

Path Through Life

Photo on page 39

Size:
9¾" across x 11" long, not including hanger.

Materials:
Two sheets of 7-count plastic canvas; Six pearl 4-mm beads; Craft glue or glue gun; Worsted-weight or plastic canvas yarn (for amounts see Color Key).

Cutting Instructions:
A: For back, cut one according to graph.
B: For front, cut one according to graph.
C: For large flowers, cut two according to graph.
D: For small flowers, cut four according to graph.
E: For leaves, cut two according to graph.
F: For stem, cut one according to graph.

Stitching Instructions:
1: Using eggshell and Continental Stitch, work A; using colors and stitches indicated, work

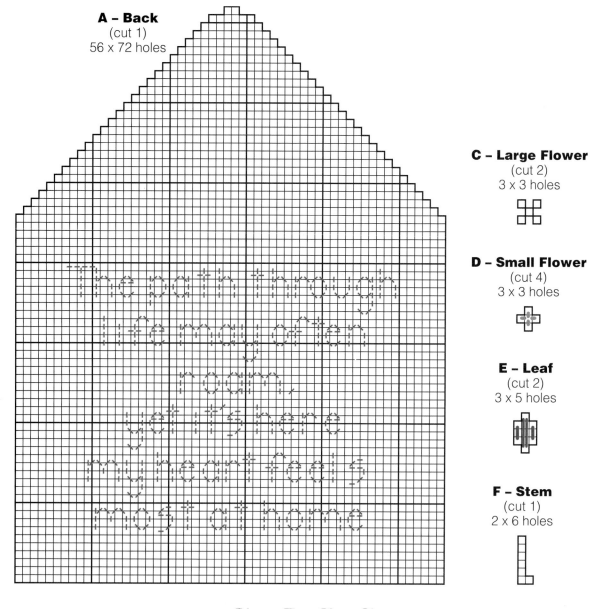

A – Back
(cut 1)
56 x 72 holes

C – Large Flower
(cut 2)
3 x 3 holes

D – Small Flower
(cut 4)
3 x 3 holes

E – Leaf
(cut 2)
3 x 5 holes

F – Stem
(cut 1)
2 x 6 holes

B, D and E pieces according to graphs. With rose, Overcast cutout edges of B; with straw for large flowers, dk. aqua for stem and with matching colors, Overcast edges of C-F pieces.

2: Using dk. aqua (separate into plies, if desired) and embroidery stitches indicated, embroider message on A as indicated on graph.

3: Holding wrong side of B to right side of A, with dk. aqua, Whipstitch matching edges together; Overcast unfinished edges of roof trim.

4: Glue stem to A at heart cutout and flowers and leaves to stem and to A as desired or as shown in photo. Glue one pearl to center of each flower.

(**Note:** Cut two 9" lengths of rose.)

5: Tie one strand into a bow, then knot each end of strand; trim ends close to knots. Glue bow to top of plaque as shown. For hanger, fold ends of remaining strand in half and glue to back of plaque at center top (see photo). ✧

COLOR KEY: Path Through Life

	Worsted-weight	Nylon Plus™	Need-loft®	YARN AMOUNT
☐	Eggshell	#24	#39	36 yds.
▨	Lt. Aqua	#39	#49	20 yds.
■	Dk. Aqua	#08	#50	13 yds.
▨	Rose	#12	#05	4 yds.
☐	Pink	#11	#07	1 yd.
☐	Straw	#41	#19	1 yd.

STITCH KEY:

— Backstitch/Straight Stitch

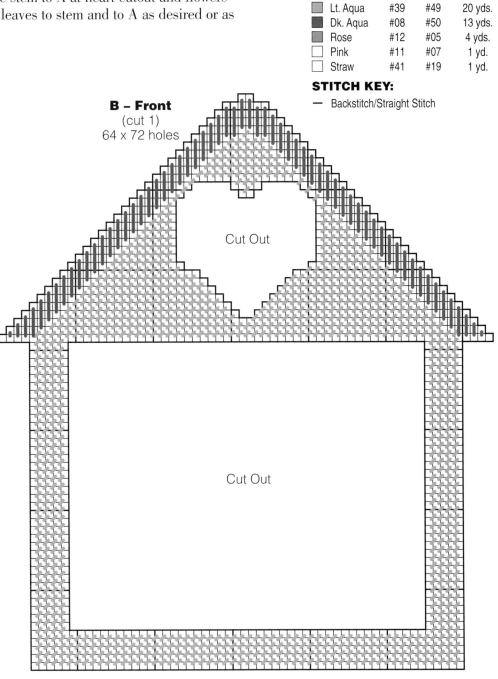

B – Front
(cut 1)
64 x 72 holes

Cut Out

Cut Out

The Nativity

Photo on page 29

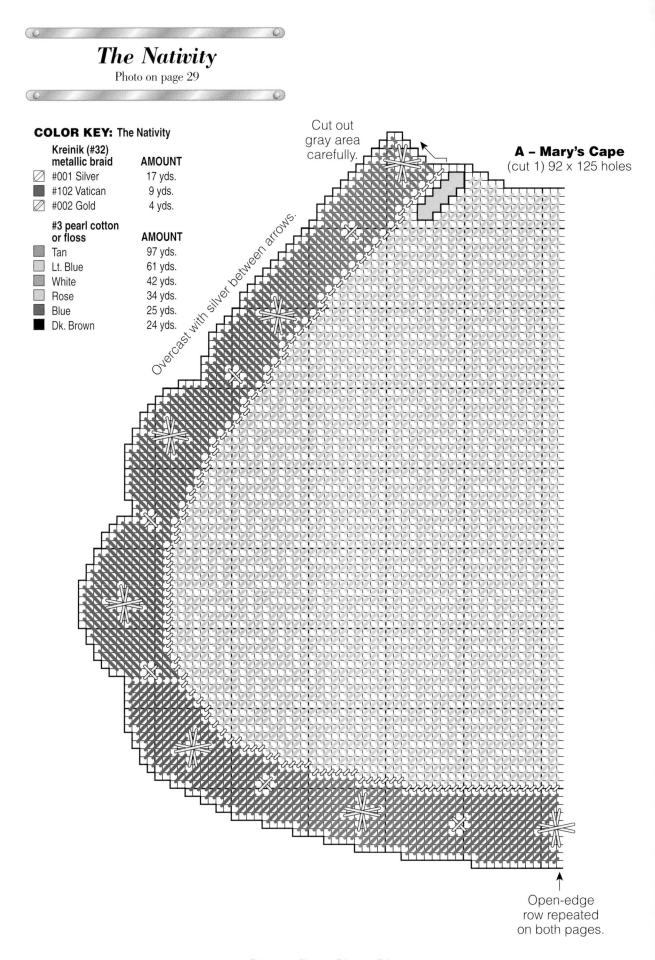

Cut out
gray area
carefully.

A – Mary's Cape
(cut 1) 92 x 125 holes

COLOR KEY: The Nativity

Kreinik (#32) metallic braid	AMOUNT
⬜ #001 Silver	17 yds.
⬛ #102 Vatican	9 yds.
⬜ #002 Gold	4 yds.

#3 pearl cotton or floss	AMOUNT
⬜ Tan	97 yds.
⬜ Lt. Blue	61 yds.
⬜ White	42 yds.
⬜ Rose	34 yds.
⬜ Blue	25 yds.
⬛ Dk. Brown	24 yds.

Overcast with silver between arrows.

Open-edge
row repeated
on both pages.

Cut out gray area carefully.

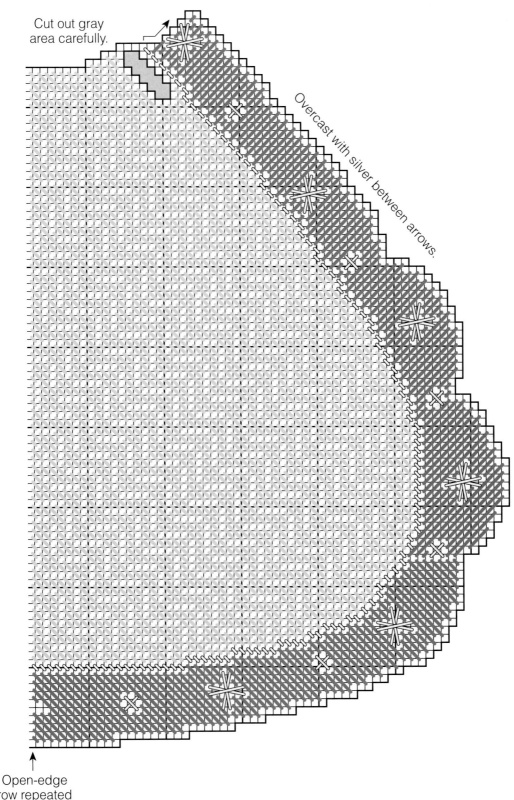

Overcast with silver between arrows.

Open-edge row repeated on both pages.

The Nativity

Photo on page 29

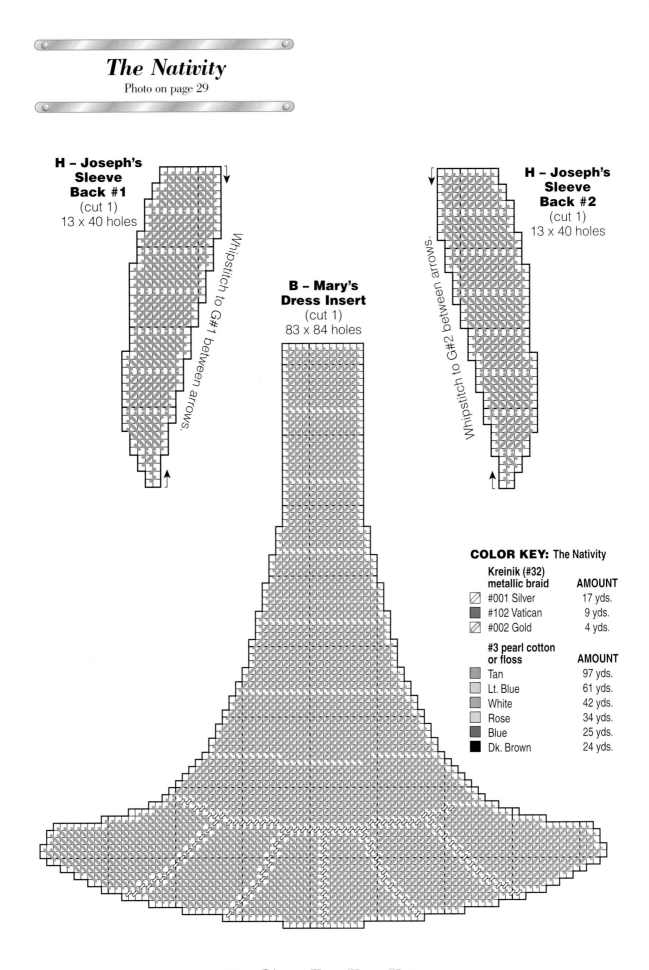

H – Joseph's Sleeve Back #1
(cut 1)
13 x 40 holes

Whipstitch to G#1 between arrows.

B – Mary's Dress Insert
(cut 1)
83 x 84 holes

H – Joseph's Sleeve Back #2
(cut 1)
13 x 40 holes

Whipstitch to G#2 between arrows.

COLOR KEY: The Nativity

Kreinik (#32) metallic braid		AMOUNT
▨	#001 Silver	17 yds.
■	#102 Vatican	9 yds.
▨	#002 Gold	4 yds.

#3 pearl cotton or floss		AMOUNT
▨	Tan	97 yds.
▨	Lt. Blue	61 yds.
▨	White	42 yds.
▨	Rose	34 yds.
▨	Blue	25 yds.
■	Dk. Brown	24 yds.

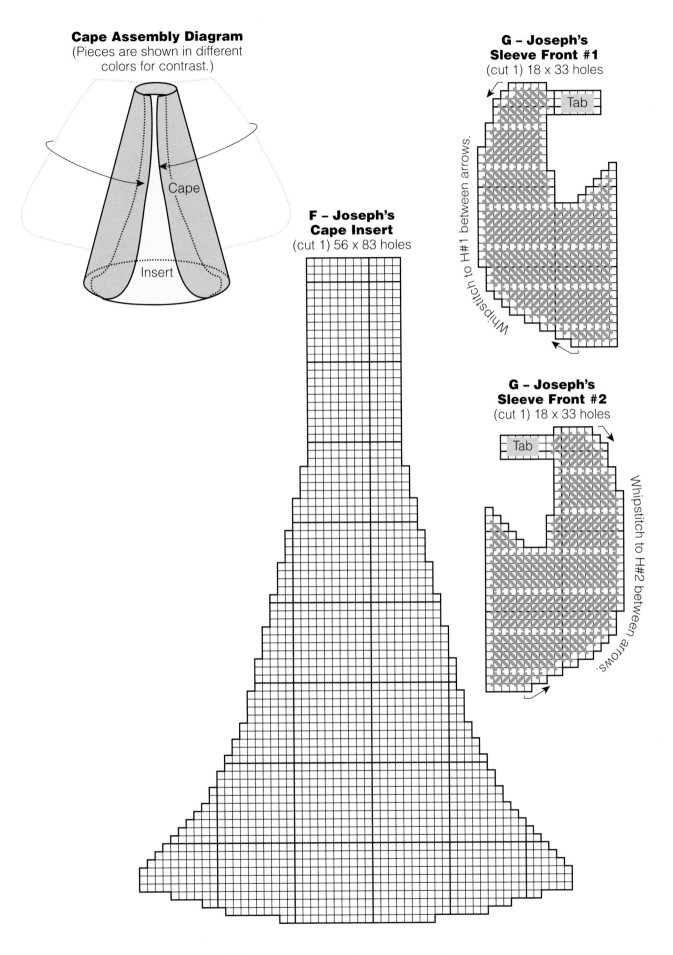

Cape Assembly Diagram
(Pieces are shown in different colors for contrast.)

Cape

Insert

**G – Joseph's
Sleeve Front #1**
(cut 1) 18 x 33 holes

Tab

Whipstitch to H#1 between arrows.

**F – Joseph's
Cape Insert**
(cut 1) 56 x 83 holes

**G – Joseph's
Sleeve Front #2**
(cut 1) 18 x 33 holes

Tab

Whipstitch to H#2 between arrows.

The Nativity

Photo on page 29

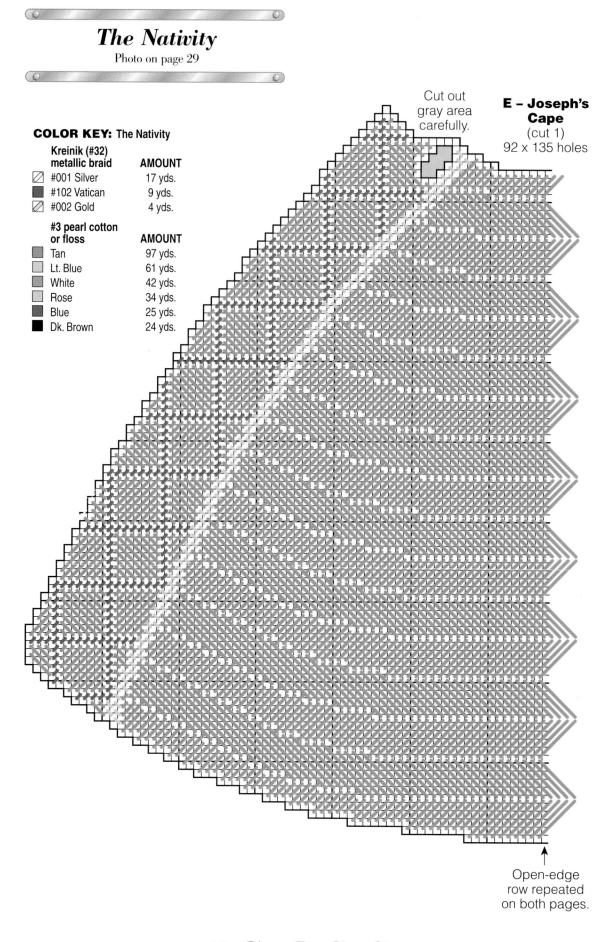

Cut out gray area carefully.

E – Joseph's Cape
(cut 1)
92 x 135 holes

Open-edge row repeated on both pages.

Cut out
gray area
carefully.

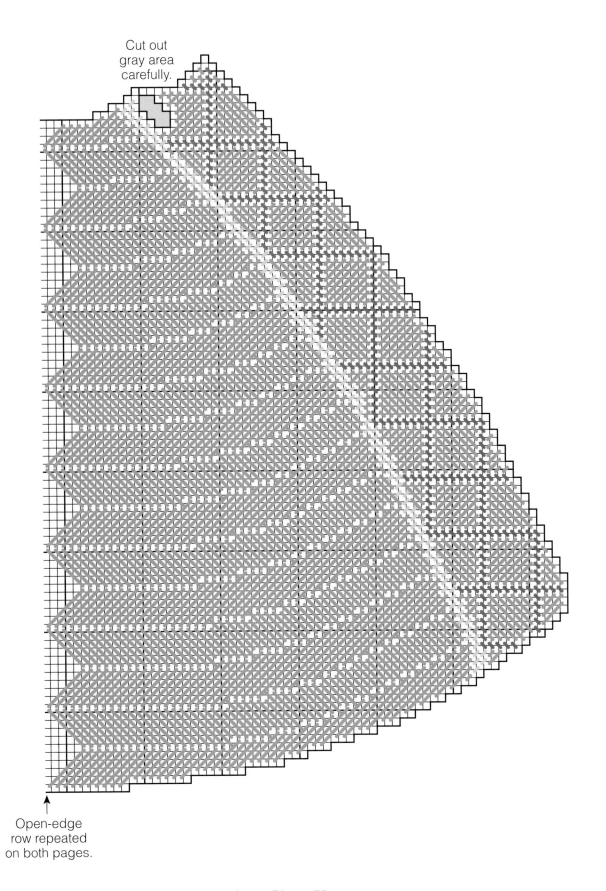

Open-edge
row repeated
on both pages.

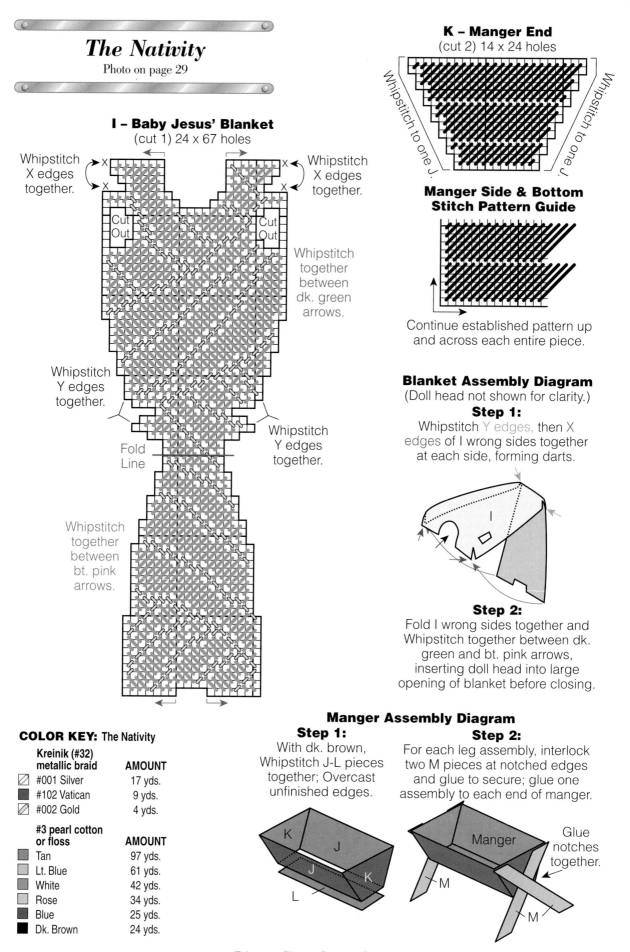

The Nativity

Photo on page 29

K – Manger End
(cut 2) 14 x 24 holes

Whipstitch to one J.

Whipstitch to one J.

Manger Side & Bottom Stitch Pattern Guide

Continue established pattern up and across each entire piece.

I – Baby Jesus' Blanket
(cut 1) 24 x 67 holes

Whipstitch X edges together.

Whipstitch X edges together.

Cut Out

Cut Out

Whipstitch together between dk. green arrows.

Whipstitch Y edges together.

Fold Line

Whipstitch Y edges together.

Whipstitch together between bt. pink arrows.

Blanket Assembly Diagram
(Doll head not shown for clarity.)

Step 1:
Whipstitch Y edges, then X edges of I wrong sides together at each side, forming darts.

Step 2:
Fold I wrong sides together and Whipstitch together between dk. green and bt. pink arrows, inserting doll head into large opening of blanket before closing.

COLOR KEY: The Nativity

Kreinik (#32) metallic braid	AMOUNT
#001 Silver	17 yds.
#102 Vatican	9 yds.
#002 Gold	4 yds.

#3 pearl cotton or floss	AMOUNT
Tan	97 yds.
Lt. Blue	61 yds.
White	42 yds.
Rose	34 yds.
Blue	25 yds.
Dk. Brown	24 yds.

Manger Assembly Diagram

Step 1:
With dk. brown, Whipstitch J-L pieces together; Overcast unfinished edges.

Step 2:
For each leg assembly, interlock two M pieces at notched edges and glue to secure; glue one assembly to each end of manger.

Glue notches together.

ULTIMATE *Fabulous Florals* **COLLECTION**

Poinsettia Doorstop

Designed by Carol Nartowicz

Size:
4¾" x 9½" x 10" tall.

Materials:
Three sheets of clear and 1½ sheets of green 7-count plastic canvas; Zip-close bag filled with sand, gravel or other weighting material; Polyester fiberfill; Craft glue or glue gun; Raffia straw (for amounts see Color Key).

Cutting Instructions:
(**Note:** Graphs continued on page 52.)

A: For base front and back, cut two (one from clear for front and one from green for back) according to graph.

B: For base upper side pieces, cut two from green 19 x 47 holes.

C: For base lower side pieces, cut two from clear according to graph.

D: For base side rim pieces, cut two from clear 3 x 19 holes.

E: For base top, cut one from green 19 x 31

holes (no graph).

F: For base bottom, cut one from clear 13 x 43 holes (no graph).

G: For large bracts/leaves, cut twenty-two from clear according to graph.

H: For small bracts/leaves, cut forty-eight from clear according to graph.

I: For flower center pieces, cut twenty-eight from clear according to graph.

Stitching Instructions:

(**Note:** Back A, E, F and twenty-one I pieces are not worked.)

1: Using gold and Long Stitch, work clear A for front and B-D pieces according to graphs. Whipstitch and assemble A-F pieces, weight and fiberfill according to Base Assembly Diagram on page 52.

2: Using colors and stitches indicated, work G (11 in red and 11 in green), H (10 in red, 21 in white and 17 in green) and seven I (four in red and three in white) pieces according to graphs. With matching colors, Overcast edges of G and H pieces.

3: Using gold and French Knot, embroider seeds on I pieces as indicated on graph. For each flower center (make 7), holding three unworked I pieces to wrong side of one worked piece, with matching color, Whipstitch together through all thicknesses.

4: Glue leaves, bracts and flower centers to front and sides of base as desired (see photo).✧

G – Large Bract/Leaf
(cut 22 from clear)
9 x 18 holes

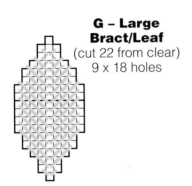

H – Small Bract/Leaf
(cut 48 from clear)
9 x 15 holes

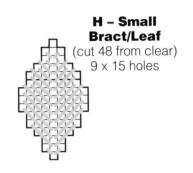

B – Base Upper Side Piece
(cut 2 from green) 19 x 47 holes

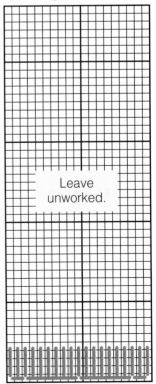

Leave unworked.

I – Flower Center Piece
(cut 28 from clear)
6 x 6 holes

D – Base Side Rim Piece
(cut 2 from clear) 3 x 19 holes

C – Base Lower Side Piece
(cut 2 from clear) 19 x 19 holes

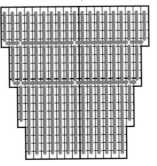

COLOR KEY: Doorstop

Raffia straw	AMOUNT
☐ Green	40 yds.
☐ Red	36 yds.
☐ White	25 yds.
▨ Gold	20 yds.
▨ Bract/Leaf Color	

STITCH KEY:
● French Knot

Poinsettia Doorstop

Photo on page 50

COLOR KEY: Doorstop

Raffia straw	AMOUNT
☐ Green	40 yds.
☐ Red	36 yds.
☐ White	25 yds.
▨ Gold	20 yds.
▨ Bract/Leaf Color	

STITCH KEY:

● French Knot

Base Assembly Diagram

Step 1:
For each side, with gold, Whipstitch one of each B-D piece together.

Step 2:
With gold, Whipstitch F and worked edges of side assemblies to A pieces.

Step 3:
Place weight in bottom; with green, Whipstitch remaining edges of assembly and E together, filling remainder of base with fiberfill before closing.

A – Base Front & Back
(cut 1 from each color) 55 x 63 holes

Leave unworked.

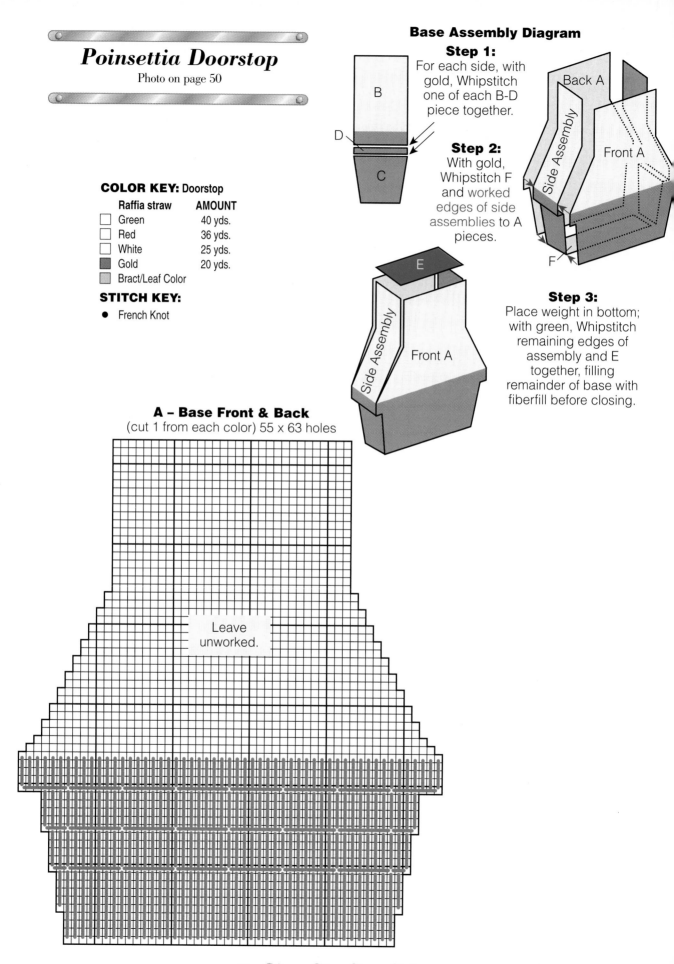

Garden Delight

Designed by Janna Britton

Size:

Coaster is 3¾" square; Mug Insert fits inside a 4" snap-together plastic mug; Napkin Holder is 2" x 6½" x 5" tall; Napkin Ring is ¾" x 1½" x 1¾".

Materials:

3¼ sheets of 14-count plastic canvas; Plastic mug with needlework insert area; 4" square piece of off-white felt (optional); White single-thick mat board (optional); Craft glue or glue gun (optional); Six-strand embroidery floss (for amounts see Color Key on page 54).

Cutting Instructions:

(**Note:** Graphs on pages 54-56.)

A: For Coaster, cut one 49 x 50 holes.

B: For Mug Insert, cut one 49 holes x desired length (no graph).

C: For Napkin Holder sides, cut two according to graph.

D: For Napkin Holder ends, cut two 11 x 26 holes.

E: For Napkin Holder bottom, cut one 26 x 90 holes (no graph).

F: For Napkin Ring band, cut one 8 x 65 holes.

G: For Napkin Ring leaves, cut one according to graph.

CONTINUED ON PAGE 54

Garden Delight

Continued from page 53

H: For Napkin Ring roses #1 and #2, cut one each according to graphs.

I: For optional Napkin Holder stability braces, using C-E pieces as patterns, cut two sides, two ends and one bottom from mat board ¼" smaller at all edges.

J: For optional Coaster backing, using A as a pattern, cut one from felt ⅛" smaller at all edges.

Stitching Instructions:

(**Notes:** E piece is not worked.)
Use Continental Stitch throughout.

1: Using six strands in colors indicated, work A-D and F-H pieces according to graphs and stitch pattern guide; fill in uncoded areas of A-D and F pieces using honey pale. With honey pale for Coaster and Mug Insert and with matching colors, Overcast edges of A, B, G and H pieces.

2: Using three strands in colors and embroidery stitches indicated, embroider detail on B-D and F pieces as indicated on graphs and stitch pattern guide.

3: Secure B in plastic mug according to manufacturer's instructions; if desired, glue J to back of Coaster.

4: Whipstitch and assemble C-E pieces as indicated and according to Napkin Holder Assembly Diagram. If desired, glue I pieces to wrong side of matching C-E pieces.

G – Napkin Ring Leaves
(cut 1)
21 x 23 holes

D – Napkin Holder End
(cut 2) 11 x 26 holes

Whipstitch to one C.

Whipstitch to one C.

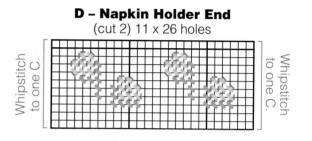

A – Coaster
(cut 1) 49 x 50 holes

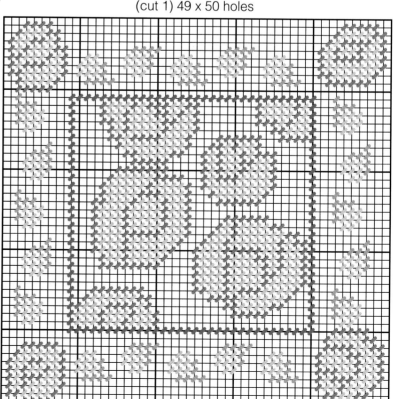

COLOR KEY: Garden Delight

DMC® embroidery floss	AMOUNT
■ #502 Sage Green Med.	31 yds.
☐ #746 Honey Pale	117 yds.
■ #961 Antique Rose Dk.	37 yds.
■ #966 Lt. Pistachio Green	17 yds.
■ #3354 Dusty Rose Lt.	17 yds.
■ White	4 yds.

STITCH KEY:

— Backstitch/Straight Stitch

● French Knot

5: With honey pale, Whipstitch short ends of F wrong sides together; with sage green med., Overcast edges. Glue roses and leaves together as shown in photo; glue assembly to F over seam, forming Napkin Ring.✧

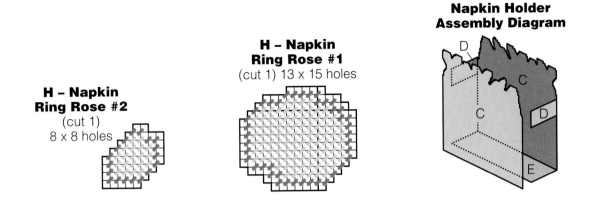

H – Napkin Ring Rose #2
(cut 1)
8 x 8 holes

H – Napkin Ring Rose #1
(cut 1) 13 x 15 holes

Napkin Holder Assembly Diagram

F – Napkin Ring Band (cut 1) 8 x 70 holes

Mug Stitch Pattern Guide

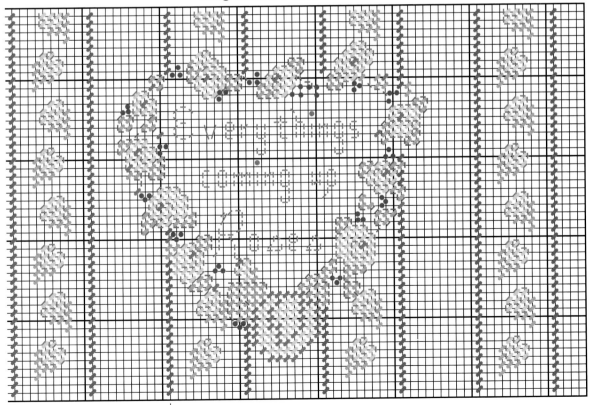

◄ Continue established striped background pattern across entire piece.

Garden Delight

Photo on page 53

COLOR KEY: Garden Delight

	DMC® embroidery floss	AMOUNT
■	#502 Sage Green Med.	31 yds.
□	#746 Honey Pale	117 yds.
■	#961 Antique Rose Dk.	37 yds.
■	#966 Lt. Pistachio Green	17 yds.
■	#3354 Dusty Rose Lt.	17 yds.
■	White	4 yds.

STITCH KEY:

— Backstitch/Straight Stitch

• French Knot

C – Napkin Holder Side
(cut 2) 68 x 90 holes

Whipstitch to one D.

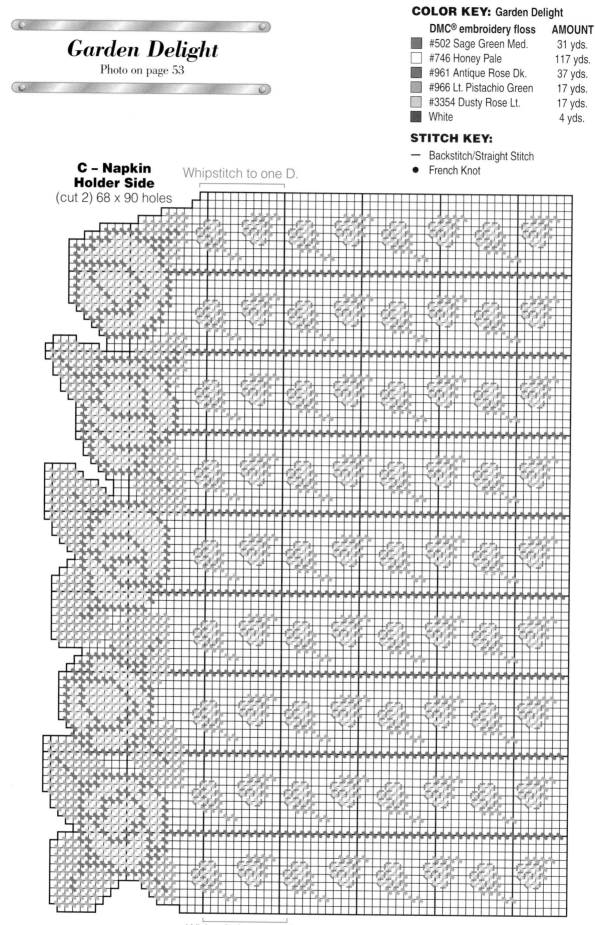

Whipstitch to one D.

Roses Are Red

Designed by Sandra Miller Maxfield

Instructions on page 58

Plant roses for those you love and fill your rooms with rich bouquets fragrant with romance.

Roses are Red

Photo on page 57

Size:
Container is 7"-square x 3½" tall; Tissue Cover is 5" x 9½" x 3¼" tall and snugly covers a 4¾" x 9½" x 3"-tall tissue box; Towel Holder is 6¾" x 8½"; Borders adjust to fit around standard acrylic bathroom accessories; each Tieback is 3¼" x 13¾" when flat. Measurements do not include embellishments.

Materials:
Seven sheets of 7-count plastic canvas; Assorted red flowers with greenery; 2 yds. gold ⅝" metallic ribbon; Craft glue or glue gun; Metallic cord (for amount see Color Key); Worsted-weight or plastic canvas yarn (for amounts see Color Key).

Cutting Instructions:
(**Note:** Graphs continued on pages 60 & 61.)

A: For Container lid top, cut one 45 x 45 holes.

B: For Container lid lip pieces, cut four 3 x 41 holes.

C: For Container box sides, cut four 21 x 43 holes.

D: For Container box bottom, cut one 43 x 43 holes (no graph).

E: For Tissue Cover top, cut one according to graph.

F: For Tissue Cover long sides, cut two 21 x 63 holes.

G: For Tissue Cover short sides, cut two 21 x 33 holes.

H: For Towel Holder front, cut one according to graph.

I: For Towel Holder bar, cut one 6 x 43 holes (no graph).

J: For Wastebasket border, cut one 21 holes x length needed to fit around basket (no graph). (**Note:** If needed, cut and overlap several pieces to achieve required length.)

K: For Cup border, cut one 15 holes x length needed to fit around cup (no graph).

L: For Candle border, cut four 15 x 20 holes.

M: For Curtain Tiebacks, cut two 21 x 90 holes (no graph).

Stitching Instructions:
(**Note:** D and I pieces are not worked.)

1: Using colors and stitches indicated, work A-C, E-H and L pieces according to graphs and work J, K (overlap holes at ends of border pieces as needed for a snug fit and work through both thicknesses at overlap areas to join) and M pieces according to Stitch Pattern Guide on page 61. With black, Overcast edges of A, J, K and M pieces and cutout edges of E and H.

2: Using cord and embroidery stitches indicated, embroider detail on A-C and E-M pieces as indicated on graphs and Stitch Pattern Guide.

3: For Container, with black, Whipstitch C and D pieces together, forming box, and Whipstitch short ends of B pieces together, forming lid lip; Overcast unfinished edges of box and lid lip. Glue lid lip to center wrong side of A.

4: For Tissue Cover, with black, Whipstitch E-G pieces together; Overcast unfinished edges.

5: For Towel Holder, holding I to wrong side of H, with black, Whipstitch together as indicated; Overcast unfinished edges of H. For candle border, Whipstitch ends of L pieces together; Overcast unfinished edges.

(**Note:** Cut four 9" lengths of ribbon.)

6: For each Tieback, glue one end of one 9" ribbon to center wrong side at each short end of one M; trim opposite end as desired.

7: Glue borders to corresponding accessory pieces; embellish Container, Tissue Cover, Towel Holder, borders and tiebacks with flowers and remaining ribbon as desired (see photo). ✧

A – Container Lid Top
(cut 1) 45 x 45 holes

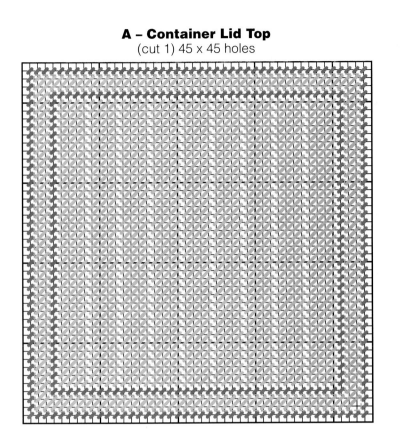

COLOR KEY: Roses Are Red

Metallic cord			AMOUNT
Gold			81 yds.

Worsted-weight	Nylon Plus™	Need-loft®	YARN AMOUNT
Black	#02	#00	7 oz.
Dk. Red	#20	#01	47 yds.
Red	#19	#02	25 yds.
Dk. Green	#31	#27	25 yds.

STITCH KEY:
— Backstitch/Straight Stitch
• French Knot

C – Container Box Side
(cut 4) 21 x 43 holes

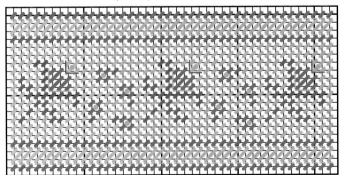

Roses are Red

Photo on page 57

E – Tissue Cover Top
(cut 1) 33 x 63 holes

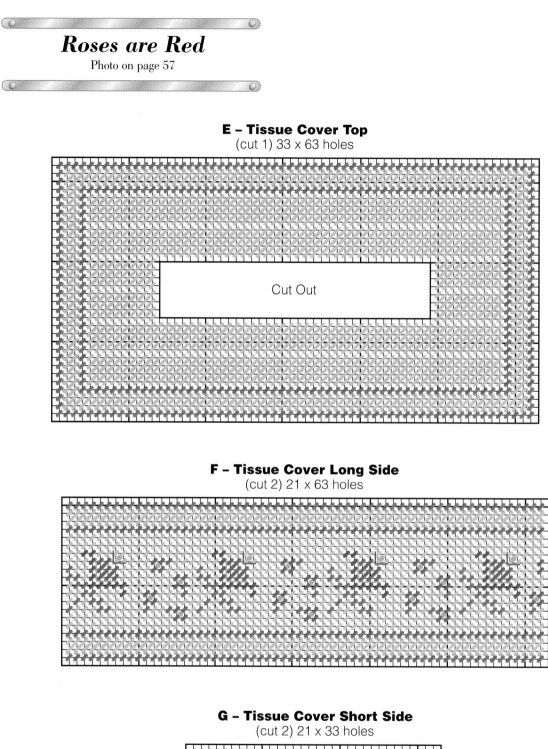

Cut Out

F – Tissue Cover Long Side
(cut 2) 21 x 63 holes

G – Tissue Cover Short Side
(cut 2) 21 x 33 holes

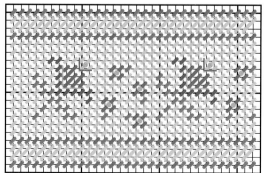

L – Candle Border
(cut 4) 15 x 20 holes

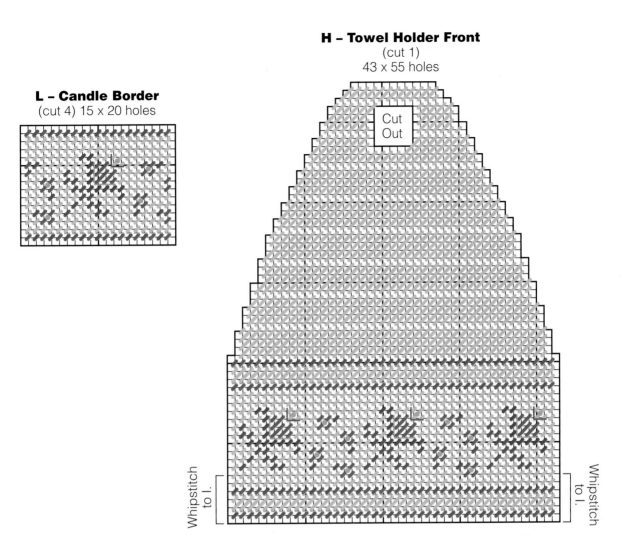

H – Towel Holder Front
(cut 1)
43 x 55 holes

Cut Out

Whipstitch to I.

Whipstitch to I.

COLOR KEY: Roses Are Red

Metallic cord			AMOUNT
Gold			81 yds.

Worsted-weight	Nylon Plus™	Need-loft®	YARN AMOUNT
Black	#02	#00	7 oz.
Dk. Red	#20	#01	47 yds.
Red	#19	#02	25 yds.
Dk. Green	#31	#27	25 yds.

STITCH KEY:

— Backstitch/Straight Stitch
● French Knot

Stitch Pattern Guide

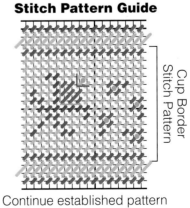

Cup Border Stitch Pattern

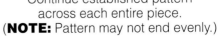

Continue established pattern
across each entire piece.
(**NOTE:** Pattern may not end evenly.)

Violets

Pansies

Summer Wind Jinglers

Designed by Vicki Blizzard

Instructions on page 64

Geraniums

Shasta Daisy

Sunflower

Hang these delightful blooms where the summer breezes can create gentle music to caress your senses.

Summer Wind Jinglers

Photo on pages 62 & 63

Size:
Each is about 6" across x 14" long, including hanger and embellishments.

Materials For One:
One sheet of 7-count plastic canvas; One Uniek® Crafts 5" plastic canvas hexagon shape (for Violets); Six to 20 gold assorted-size jingle bells; Two to four yds. coordinating color ⅛" to ¼" satin ribbon; Craft glue or glue gun; #3 pearl cotton or six-strand embroidery floss (for amount see individual Color Keys on pages 66-68); Worsted-weight or plastic canvas yarn (for amounts see individual Color Keys).

Pansies
Cutting Instructions:
(**Note:** Graphs & diagrams on page 66.)
A: For small petals, cut twelve according to graph.
B: For medium petals, cut twelve according to graph.
C: For large petals, cut six according to graph.
D: For leaves, cut four according to graph.
E: For flower centers, cut six according to graph.

Stitching Instructions:
1: Using mint and stitches indicated, work D pieces according to graph; using Continental Stitch, work four A, four B and two C pieces in each of the following colors: watermelon, white and yellow. Using yellow and Continental Stitch, work E pieces. With matching colors, Overcast edges of A-E pieces.
2: Using pearl cotton or six strands floss and Straight Stitch, embroider detail on B and C pieces as indicated on graphs.
3: For each pansy (make two of each color),

glue matching-color A-C pieces together according to Pansy Assembly Diagram. For each pansy bouquet (make two; reverse placement of white and yellow pansy on one side), glue one of each color pansy, two D and three E pieces together according to Pansy Bouquet Assembly Diagram.
(**Note:** Cut ten 12" and four 6" lengths of ribbon.)
4: For each tassel (make two), tie one 6" ribbon around center of five 12" ribbons; fold ribbons in half, and securing ends under wraps as you work, wrap one 6" ribbon around fold. Glue one tassel to wrong side of each leaf one on pansy side.
(**Note:** Cut one 12" length of ribbon.)
5: For hanger, glue one end of 12" ribbon to back of one white pansy and opposite end to back of adjacent yellow pansy.
6: Glue bouquets wrong sides together at matching edges. Secure bells to ends of tassel tails as desired (see photo).

Sunflower
Cutting Instructions:
(**Note:** Graphs & diagram on page 66.)
A: For flower centers, cut two according to graph.
B: For small petals, cut twenty-four according to graph.
C: For large petals, cut sixteen according to graph.

Stitching Instructions:
1: Using colors and stitches indicated, work pieces according to graphs; with matching colors, Overcast edges.
2: Using dk. brown and French Knot, embroider seeds on A as indicated on graph.
3: For each sunflower (make two), glue one A, twelve B and eight C pieces together according to Sunflower Assembly Diagram.
(**Note:** Cut six 12" and one 6" length of ribbon.)
4: Follow tassel instructions in Step 4 of Pansies to make one tassel. Glue tassel to wrong side of one sunflower; glue ends of remaining 12" ribbon to wrong side of same sunflower, forming hanger. Glue sunflower centers wrong sides together. Secure bells to ends of tassel tails as desired (see photo).

Violets

Cutting Instructions:

(**Note:** Graphs & diagrams on page 67.)

A: For bases, cut two from hexagon shape according to graph.

B: For front petals, cut eight according to graph.

C: For back petals, cut eight according to graph.

D: For leaves, cut eight according to Pansies D graph.

Stitching Instructions:

1: Using colors and stitches indicated, work pieces according to graphs; with matching colors, Overcast edges.

2: Using pearl cotton or six strands floss and French Knot, embroider flower centers on B pieces as indicated on graph.

3: For each violet (make eight), glue one of each B and C together according to Violet Assembly Diagram; for each violets bouquet (make two), glue one A, four D and four violets together according to Violets Bouquet Assembly Diagram.

(**Note:** Cut five 12" and one 6" length of ribbon.)

4: For tassel, tie 6" ribbon around center of four 12" ribbons. Glue tassel to wrong side of one violet bouquet at one base end point; glue ends of remaining 12" ribbon to wrong side of base at opposite end point, forming hanger (see photo).

5: Glue bouquets wrong sides together at matching edges. Secure bells to ends of tassel tails as desired (see photo).

Geraniums

Cutting Instructions:

(**Note:** Graphs & diagrams on pages 67 & 68.)

A: For bases, cut two according to graph.

B: For flower petals, cut seventy according to graph.

C: For flower centers, cut fourteen according to graph.

D: For flower buds, cut ten according to graph.

Stitching Instructions:

1: Using colors and stitches indicated, work pieces according to graphs; with matching colors, Overcast edges.

2: Using yellow and French Knot, embroider seeds on C pieces as indicated on graph.

3: For each geranium (make 14), glue five B pieces and one C together according to Geranium Assembly Diagram; for each geraniums bouquet (make two), glue one A, four D and seven geraniums together according to Geraniums Bouquet Assembly Diagram.

(**Note:** Cut eight 12" lengths of ribbon.)

4: Glue one end of seven ribbons evenly spaced to wrong side at one straight edge of one base (see photo); trim opposite ends to desired lengths. Glue ends of remaining ribbon to wrong side of same base, forming hanger.

5: Glue remaining D pieces wrong sides together over end of center ribbon tail as shown in photo and secure bells to ends of tassel tails as desired (see photo).

Shasta Daisy

Cutting Instructions:

(**Note:** Graphs & diagram on page 68.)

A: For flower centers, cut two according to graph.

B: For small petals, cut sixteen according to graph.

C: For large petals, cut sixteen according to graph.

Stitching Instructions:

1: Using colors and stitches indicated, work pieces according to graphs; with matching colors, Overcast edges.

2: Using yellow and French Knot, embroider seeds on A pieces as indicated on graph.

3: For each daisy (make two), glue one A and eight of each B and C together according to Daisy Assembly Diagram.

(**Note:** Cut five 12" and one 6" length of ribbon.)

4: For tassel, tie 6" ribbon around center of four 12" ribbons. Glue tassel to wrong side of one daisy; glue ends of remaining 12" ribbon to wrong side of same daisy, forming hanger (see photo).

5: Glue daisy flower centers wrong sides together. Secure bells to ends of tassel tails as desired (see photo). ❖

Summer Wind Jinglers

Photo on pages 62 & 63

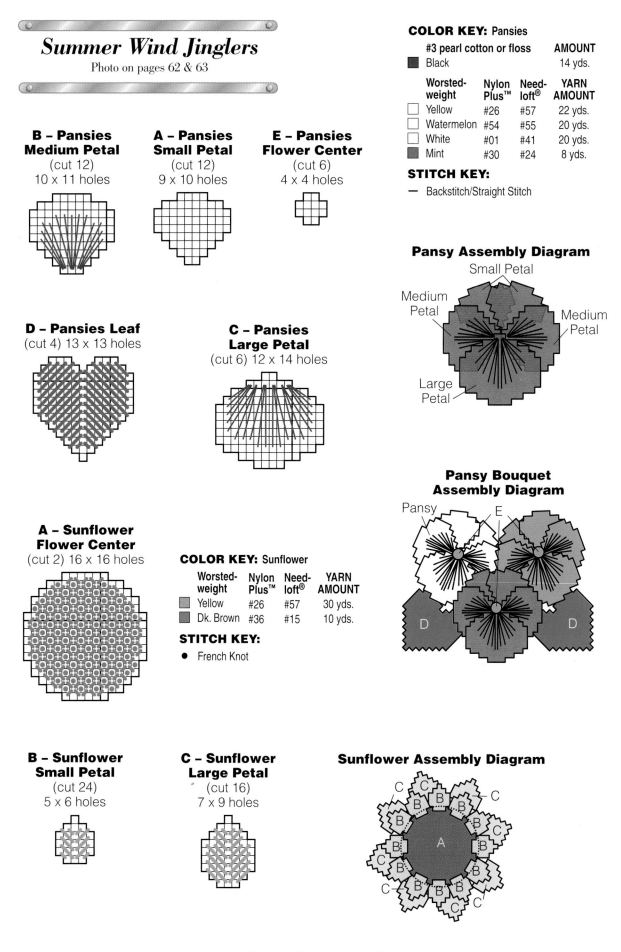

COLOR KEY: Pansies

#3 pearl cotton or floss			AMOUNT
■ Black			14 yds.

Worsted-weight	Nylon Plus™	Need-loft®	YARN AMOUNT
□ Yellow	#26	#57	22 yds.
□ Watermelon	#54	#55	20 yds.
□ White	#01	#41	20 yds.
■ Mint	#30	#24	8 yds.

STITCH KEY:
— Backstitch/Straight Stitch

B – Pansies Medium Petal
(cut 12)
10 x 11 holes

A – Pansies Small Petal
(cut 12)
9 x 10 holes

E – Pansies Flower Center
(cut 6)
4 x 4 holes

Pansy Assembly Diagram

Small Petal
Medium Petal
Medium Petal
Large Petal

D – Pansies Leaf
(cut 4) 13 x 13 holes

C – Pansies Large Petal
(cut 6) 12 x 14 holes

Pansy Bouquet Assembly Diagram

Pansy
E
D
D

A – Sunflower Flower Center
(cut 2) 16 x 16 holes

COLOR KEY: Sunflower

Worsted-weight	Nylon Plus™	Need-loft®	YARN AMOUNT
Yellow	#26	#57	30 yds.
Dk. Brown	#36	#15	10 yds.

STITCH KEY:
● French Knot

B – Sunflower Small Petal
(cut 24)
5 x 6 holes

C – Sunflower Large Petal
(cut 16)
7 x 9 holes

Sunflower Assembly Diagram

C C C
C
B B B
B
B
C
A
B
B
C
B B B B
C C

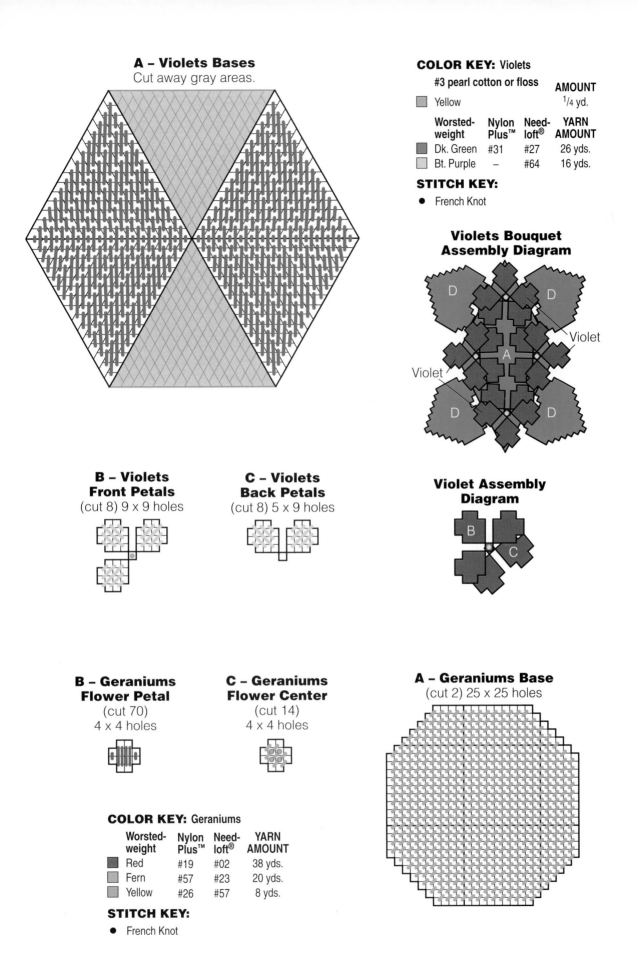

A – Violets Bases
Cut away gray areas.

COLOR KEY: Violets

#3 pearl cotton or floss			AMOUNT
▓ Yellow			¼ yd.

Worsted-weight	Nylon Plus™	Need-loft®	YARN AMOUNT
■ Dk. Green	#31	#27	26 yds.
▒ Bt. Purple	–	#64	16 yds.

STITCH KEY:
- French Knot

Violets Bouquet Assembly Diagram

Violet

Violet

B – Violets Front Petals
(cut 8) 9 x 9 holes

C – Violets Back Petals
(cut 8) 5 x 9 holes

Violet Assembly Diagram

B – Geraniums Flower Petal
(cut 70)
4 x 4 holes

C – Geraniums Flower Center
(cut 14)
4 x 4 holes

A – Geraniums Base
(cut 2) 25 x 25 holes

COLOR KEY: Geraniums

Worsted-weight	Nylon Plus™	Need-loft®	YARN AMOUNT
■ Red	#19	#02	38 yds.
▒ Fern	#57	#23	20 yds.
▒ Yellow	#26	#57	8 yds.

STITCH KEY:
- French Knot

Summer Wind Jinglers

Photo on pages 62 & 63

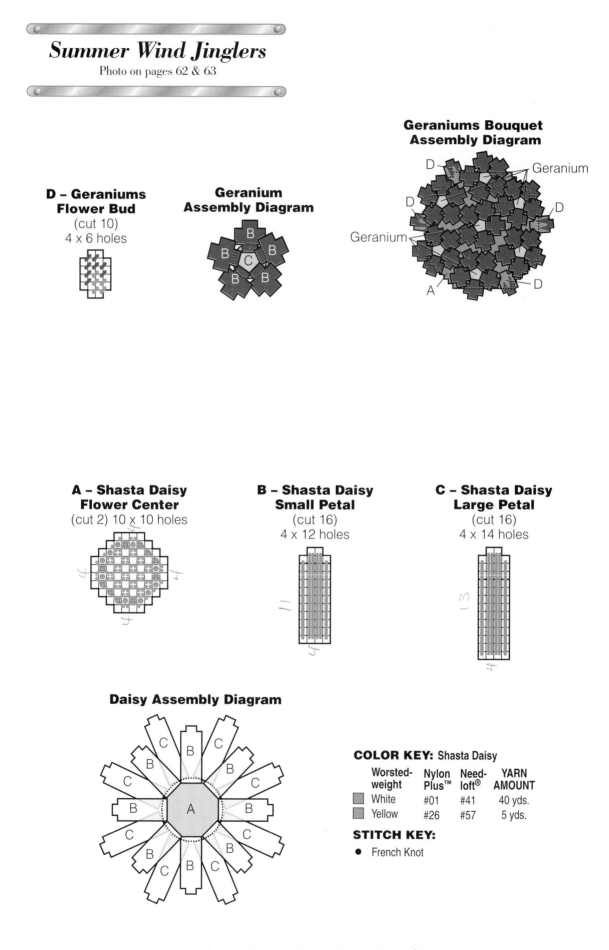

D – Geraniums Flower Bud
(cut 10)
4 x 6 holes

Geranium Assembly Diagram

Geraniums Bouquet Assembly Diagram

D
Geranium
D
Geranium
D
A
D

A – Shasta Daisy Flower Center
(cut 2) 10 x 10 holes

B – Shasta Daisy Small Petal
(cut 16)
4 x 12 holes

C – Shasta Daisy Large Petal
(cut 16)
4 x 14 holes

Daisy Assembly Diagram

COLOR KEY: Shasta Daisy

	Worsted-weight	Nylon Plus™	Need-loft®	YARN AMOUNT
	White	#01	#41	40 yds.
	Yellow	#26	#57	5 yds.

STITCH KEY:
- French Knot

ULTIMATE

Star Spangled Summer

COLLECTION

Bright Sails Trio

Designed by Glenda Chamberlain

Size:

Tote is 2⅞" x 11" x 12⅜"; Eyeglasses Case holds a standard pair of eyeglasses; Can Cozy is 2¾" across x 4¼" tall.

Materials:

Five sheets of 7-count plastic canvas; One 3" plastic canvas radial circle; Worsted-weight or plastic canvas yarn (for amounts see Color Key).

Cutting Instructions:

(**Note:** Graphs continued on page 72.)
A: For Tote sides, cut two according to graph.
B: For Tote ends, cut two 18 x 64 holes.

C: For Tote bottom, cut one 18 x 72 holes (no graph).
D: For Eyeglasses Case, cut one according to graph.
E: For Can Cozy, cut one 27 x 63 holes.
F: For Can Cozy bottom, use 3" circle (no graph).

Stitching Instructions:

(**Note:** C and F pieces are not worked.)
1: Using colors and stitches indicated, work A, B, D and E (overlap four holes at ends of E and work through both thicknesses at overlap areas to join) according to graphs and Can Cozy Stitch Pattern Guide on page 72.
2: With matching colors, Whipstitch A-C pieces together according to Tote Assembly Diagram on page 72; Overcast unfinished edges.
3: For Eyeglasses Case, folding D wrong sides together, with dk. red, Whipstitch together as indicated on graph; Overcast unfinished edges.
4: For Can Cozy, with dk. red, Whipstitch E and F pieces together; Overcast unfinished edges. ✧

B – Tote End
(cut 2) 18 x 64 holes

COLOR KEY: Bright Sails Trio

Worsted-weight	Nylon Plus™	Need-loft®	YARN AMOUNT
Royal	#09	#32	3½ oz.
White	#01	#41	75 yds.
Dk. Red	#20	#01	60 yds.
Dk. Green	#31	#27	6 yds.
Dk. Orange	#18	#52	5 yds.
Lemon	#25	#20	5 yds.

D – Eyeglasses Case
(cut 1) 46 x 48 holes

Whipstitch between arrows.

Bright Sails Trio

Photo on page 70

Tote Assembly Diagram

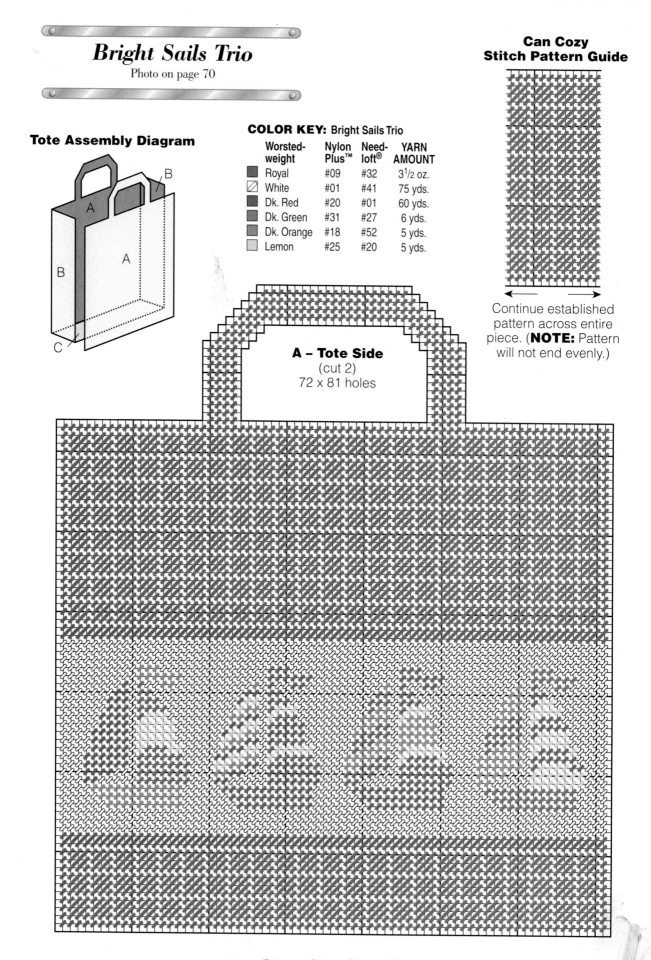

COLOR KEY: Bright Sails Trio

Worsted-weight	Nylon Plus™	Need-loft®	YARN AMOUNT
■ Royal	#09	#32	3¹/₂ oz.
▨ White	#01	#41	75 yds.
■ Dk. Red	#20	#01	60 yds.
■ Dk. Green	#31	#27	6 yds.
■ Dk. Orange	#18	#52	5 yds.
▨ Lemon	#25	#20	5 yds.

Can Cozy Stitch Pattern Guide

Continue established pattern across entire piece. (**NOTE:** Pattern will not end evenly.)

A – Tote Side
(cut 2)
72 x 81 holes

Spiraling Star

Designed by Ruby Thacker

Instructions on page 74

Spiraling Star

Photo on page 73

Size:
12¾" across x 33" long.

Materials:
Seven sheets of 7-count plastic canvas; One gold size 3/0 barrel swivel (available where fishing equipment is sold); 18 clear 4- x 6-mm pony beads; Metallic cord (for amount see Color Key); Worsted-weight or plastic canvas yarn (for amounts see Color Key).

Cutting Instructions:
A: For roof top pieces, cut six according to graph.

B: For roof bottom, cut one according to graph.

C: For roof sides, cut six 6 x 42 holes.

D: For star sides, cut thirty-six according to graph.

Stitching Instructions:
(**Note:** B piece is not worked.)

1: Using purple and stitches indicated, work one A, one C and six D pieces according to graphs; substituting orange, royal, yellow, dk. red and dk. green for purple, work one A, one C and six D pieces in each color according to graphs.

(**Note:** Cut eighteen 22" lengths of cord; tie a knot in one end of each strand.)

2: For each star, holding two matching color D pieces wrong sides together with knotted end of one cord strand between, with matching color, Whipstitch together.

3: With cord, Whipstitch and assemble star strands, beads and A-C pieces as indicated on graphs and according to Mobile Assembly Diagram on page 88.

4: For hanger, thread a strand of cord through center top of roof and through one ring on swivel; tie ends together in a knot to secure. ✧

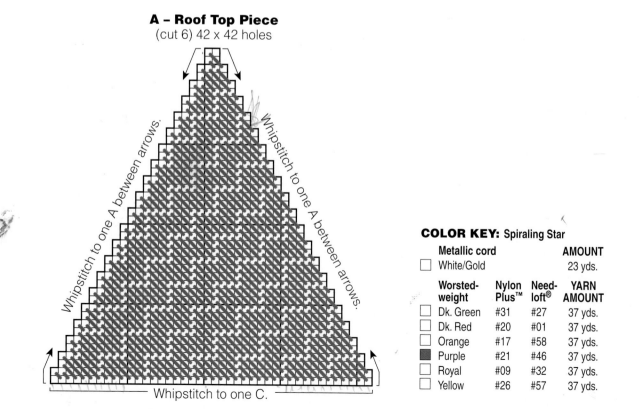

A – Roof Top Piece
(cut 6) 42 x 42 holes

Whipstitch to one A between arrows.

Whipstitch to one A between arrows.

Whipstitch to one C.

COLOR KEY: Spiraling Star

Metallic cord			AMOUNT
☐ White/Gold			23 yds.

Worsted-weight	Nylon Plus™	Need-loft®	YARN AMOUNT
☐ Dk. Green	#31	#27	37 yds.
☐ Dk. Red	#20	#01	37 yds.
☐ Orange	#17	#58	37 yds.
■ Purple	#21	#46	37 yds.
☐ Royal	#09	#32	37 yds.
☐ Yellow	#26	#57	37 yds.

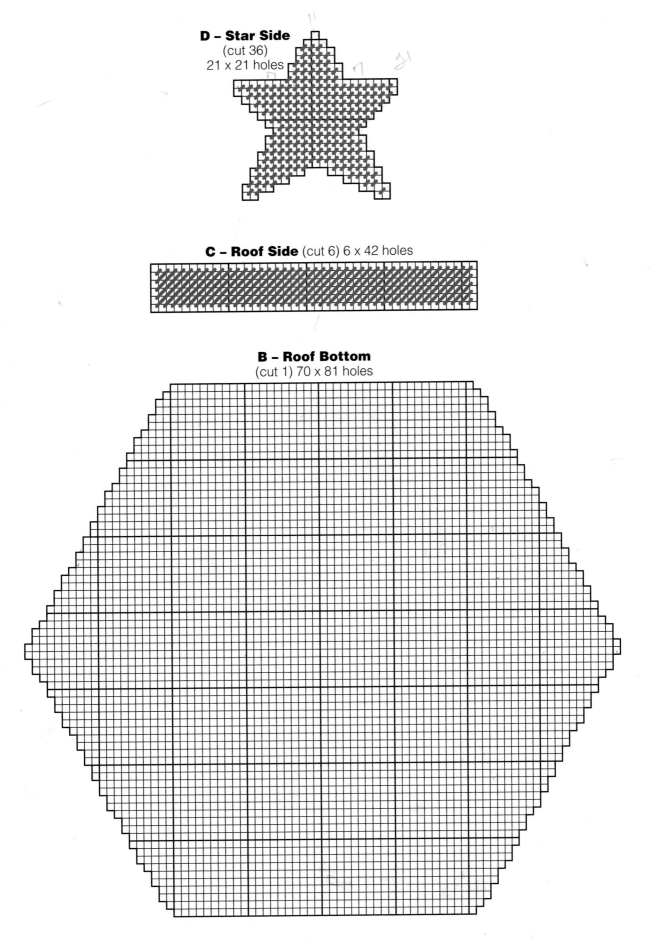

D – Star Side
(cut 36)
21 x 21 holes

C – Roof Side (cut 6) 6 x 42 holes

B – Roof Bottom
(cut 1) 70 x 81 holes

Batter Up!

Designed by Mary T. Cosgrove

Size:
8½" across x 7⅝" tall.

Materials:
Two sheets of bright blue 7-count plastic canvas; One 9½" plastic canvas radial circle; Worsted-weight or plastic canvas yarn (for amounts see Color Key).

Cutting Instructions:
A: For side pieces, cut two 50 x 90 holes.
B: For bottom, cut away outer three rows of holes from 9½" circle (no graph).

Stitching Instructions:
(Note: B piece is not worked.)
1: Using colors indicated and Continental Stitch, omitting yellow trim and leaving uncoded areas unworked, work one A according to graph.
2: Overlapping short ends of A pieces as indicated on graph, with bt. blue, Whipstitch together through all thicknesses at overlap

areas to join.

3: Using bt. yellow and stitches indicated and working over seams, work trim around entire side according to graph.

4: With bt. blue, Whipstitch A and B pieces together; do not Overcast unfinished edges.✧

COLOR KEY: Batter Up!

	Worsted-weight	Nylon Plus™	Need-loft®	YARN AMOUNT
Red		#19	#02	8 yds.
Bt. Blue		–	#60	7 yds.
Bt. Yellow		–	#63	5 yds.
White		#01	#41	4 yds.
Black		#02	#00	2 yds.
Maple		#35	#13	2 yds.
Coral		#14	#66	1 yd.

A – Side Piece
(cut 2) 50 x 90 holes

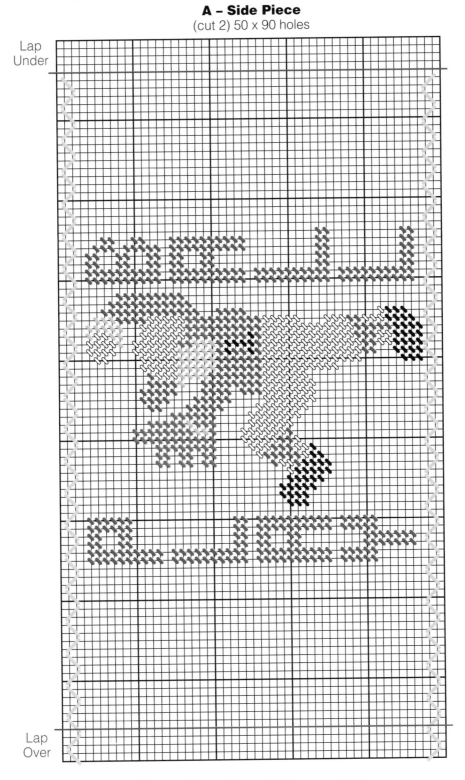

Lap Under

Lap Over

Fancy Farm Animals

Designed by Vicki Blizzard

Size:
Each is 3" across, not including embellishments.

Materials For One:
One Darice® 3" plastic canvas radial circle; Scraps of 7-count plastic canvas; Two black 12-mm half-round cabochons; One 3"-square piece of white felt; Magnetic strips; ¼ yd. coordinating-color ⅛-¼" satin ribbon (for Cow or Duck); One copper ⅝" cow bell (for Cow); Craft glue or glue gun; Worsted-weight or plastic canvas yarn (for amounts see individual Color Keys on pages 80 & 81).

(**Note:** Graphs & diagrams on pages 80 & 81.)

Chicken
Cutting Instructions:
A: For head, use 3" circle (no graph).
B: For cheeks, cut two according to graph.

C: For beak pieces, cut three 5 x 5 holes.

D: For wattle, cut one according to graph.

E: For comb center and end pieces, cut number indicated according to graphs.

F: For leaves, cut two according to graph.

G: For flower, cut one according to graph.

Stitching Instructions:

(**Note:** One C piece is not worked.)

1: Using colors and stitches indicated, work A, B, two C and D-F pieces according to stitch pattern guide and graphs; with white for flower and with matching colors, Overcast edges of A, B and D-G pieces.

2: Using yellow and French Knot, embroider flower center on G as indicated on graph.

3: With tangerine, Whipstitch C pieces together according to Beak Assembly Diagram; Overcast unfinished edges.

(**Note:** Cut one 3" circle from felt.)

4: Glue felt, magnetic strips and comb pieces (see photo) to back of head; glue beak, cheeks, wattle, leaves, flower and cabochons to front of head (see photo).

Sheep

Cutting Instructions:

A: For head, use 3" circle (no graph).

B: For cheeks, cut two according to Chicken B graph.

C: For muzzle, cut one according to graph.

D: For ears, cut one each according to graphs.

E: For leaves, cut five according to Chicken F graph.

F: For flowers, cut nine according to graph.

Stitching Instructions:

1: Using colors and stitches indicated, work A-E pieces according to stitch pattern guide and graphs. With white for ears and with matching colors, Overcast edges of A-E pieces; with lt. pink, lt. yellow and sail blue, Overcast three F pieces in each color.

2: Using lt. pink and embroidery stitches indicated, embroider mouth and nose detail on C as indicated on graph.

(**Note:** Cut one 3" circle from felt.)

3: Glue felt and magnetic strips to back of head; glue ears, cheeks, muzzle, leaves, flowers and cabochons to front of head (see photo).

Duck

Cutting Instructions:

A: For head, use 3" circle (no graph).

B: For cheeks, cut two according to Chicken B graph.

C: For beak pieces, cut two according to graph.

D: For leaves, cut five according to Chicken F graph.

E: For flowers, cut five according to graph.

Stitching Instructions:

1: Using colors and stitches indicated, work A-D pieces according to stitch pattern guide and graphs; with peach for flowers and with matching colors, Overcast edges of A, B, D and E pieces.

2: Using white and French Knot, embroider flower centers on E pieces as indicated on graph.

3: For each beak piece, with yellow, Whipstitch Y edges of one C piece wrong sides together as indicated; Overcast unfinished edges.

(**Notes:** Cut one 4" length of white; cut one 3" circle from felt.

Tie ribbon into a small bow; trim ends.

4: For hair, attach white strand through one hole at top edge of A with a Lark's Head Knot. Pull ends to even; trim and fray ends to fluff. Glue felt and magnetic strips to back of head. Holding C pieces wrong sides together, glue to head as indicated on C graph; with hair at center top, glue leaves, bow, cheeks, flowers and cabochons to front of head (see photo).

Pig

Cutting Instructions:

A: For head, use 3" circle (no graph).

B: For cheeks, cut two according to Chicken B graph.

C: For snout pieces, cut five according to graph.

D: For mouth pieces, cut one each according to graphs.

E: For ears, cut two according to graph.

F: For bandanna, cut one according to graph.

G: For bandanna ties, cut two according to graph.

CONTINUED ON PAGE 80

Patriotic Picnic Set

Designed by Robin Howard Will

Size:
Place Mat is 10½" x 13¾";
Utensil Caddy is 6" across x 10"
tall, including handle.

Materials:
Four sheets of clear and ½ sheet of white
7-count plastic canvas; 1½ yds. gold ⅝"
metallic ribbon; Craft glue or glue gun;
Metallic cord (for amount see Color Key on
page 87); Worsted-weight or plastic canvas yarn
(for amounts see Color Key).

Cutting Instructions:
(**Notes:** Graphs on pages 86 & 87.
Use white for E and F and clear canvas for
remaining pieces.)
A: For Place Mat front and lining, cut two (one
for front and one for lining) according to
graph.
B: For Utensil Caddy side pieces, cut two 30 x
65 holes (no graph).
C: For Utensil Caddy bottom, cut one according to graph.
D: For Utensil Caddy handle, cut one according to graph.

E: For Utensil Caddy divider section #1, cut
one according to graph.
F: For Utensil Caddy divider section #2, cut
one according to graph.

Stitching Instructions:
(**Note:** Lining A, C, E and F pieces are not
worked.)
1: Using colors and stitches indicated, work
one A for front, B (overlap short ends of
each piece one hole and work through both
thicknesses at overlap areas to join) and D
pieces according to graphs and stitch pattern guide on page 88. With red, Overcast
edges of E and F pieces.
2: Using cord and Backstitch, embroider star
outlines on front A as indicated on graph.
3: For Place Mat, holding lining A to wrong
side of worked piece, with cord, Whipstitch
together.
4: For Utensil Caddy, Whipstitch and assemble B-F pieces according to Caddy Assembly Diagram on page 88.
(**Note:** Cut two 9½", two 6" and six 3½"
lengths of ribbon.)
5: For each bow (make two), glue one of each
size ribbon together according to Bow
Assembly Diagram. For each bow tail (make
four), trim one end of one 3½" ribbon as
desired. Glue two tails and one bow to each
side seam on Utensil Caddy (see photo). ✧

Bow Assembly Diagram

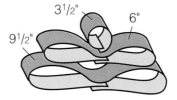

*Let the fireworks begin
when you celebrate
Independence Day with
star-studded cookout accents.*

A – Place Mat Front & Lining
(cut 1 each) 69 x 90 holes

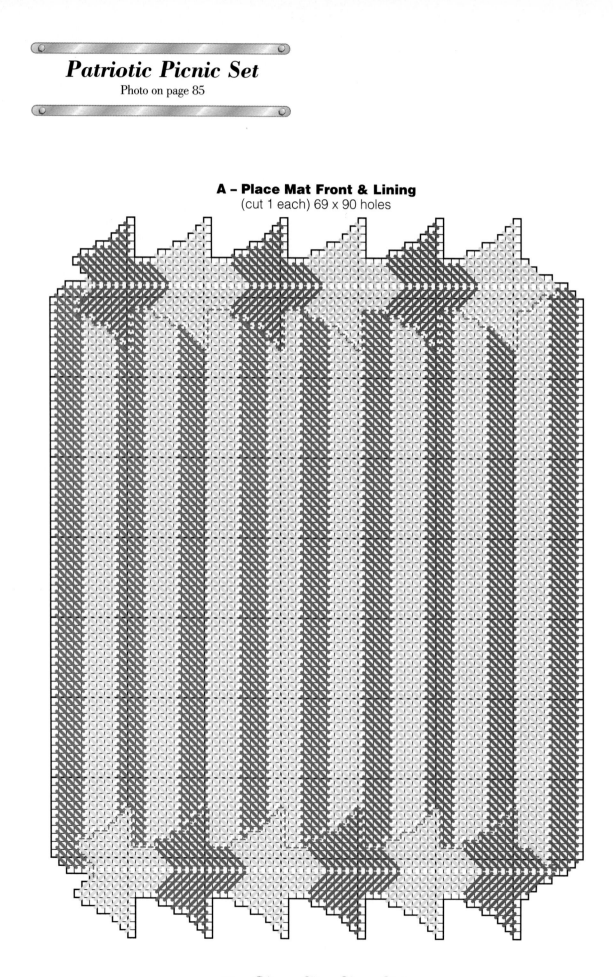

COLOR KEY: Patriotic Picnic Set

Metallic cord			AMOUNT
▨ Gold			16 yds.

Worsted-weight	Nylon Plus™	Need-loft®	YARN AMOUNT
☐ White	#01	#41	85 yds.
▨ Red	#19	#02	60 yds.
▨ Royal	#09	#32	25 yds.

STITCH KEY:
— Backstitch/Straight Stitch

C – Utensil Caddy Bottom
(cut 1) 39 x 39 holes

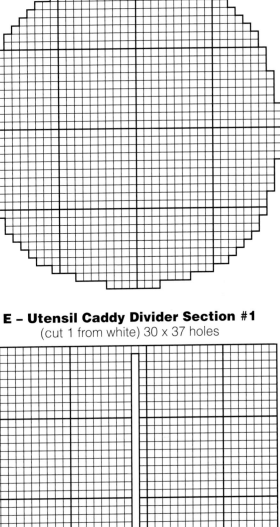

D – Utensil Caddy Handle
(cut 1) 17 x 86 holes

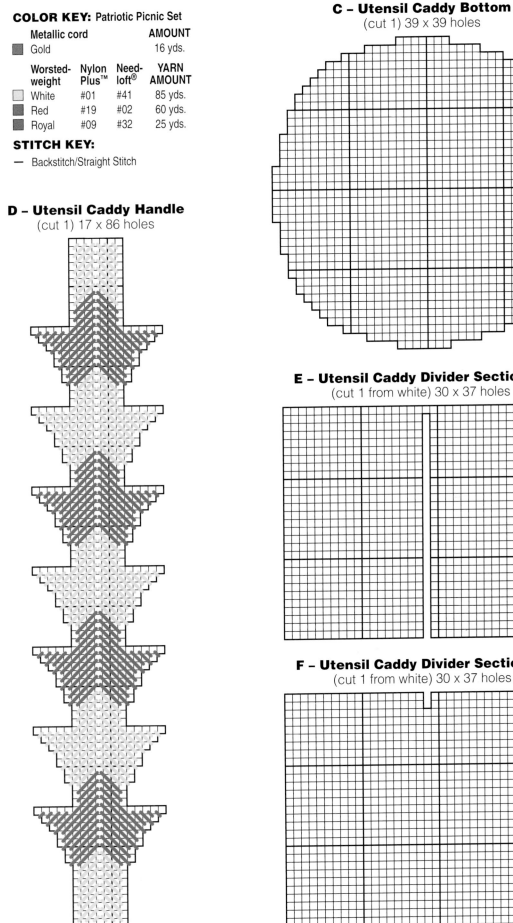

E – Utensil Caddy Divider Section #1
(cut 1 from white) 30 x 37 holes

F – Utensil Caddy Divider Section #2
(cut 1 from white) 30 x 37 holes

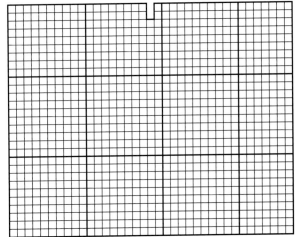

Patriotic Picnic Set

Photo on page 85

COLOR KEY: Patriotic Picnic Set

Metallic cord			AMOUNT
Gold			16 yds.

Worsted-weight	Nylon Plus™	Need-loft®	YARN AMOUNT
White	#01	#41	85 yds.
Red	#19	#02	60 yds.
Royal	#09	#32	25 yds.

STITCH KEY:

— Backstitch/Straight Stitch

Stitch Pattern Guide

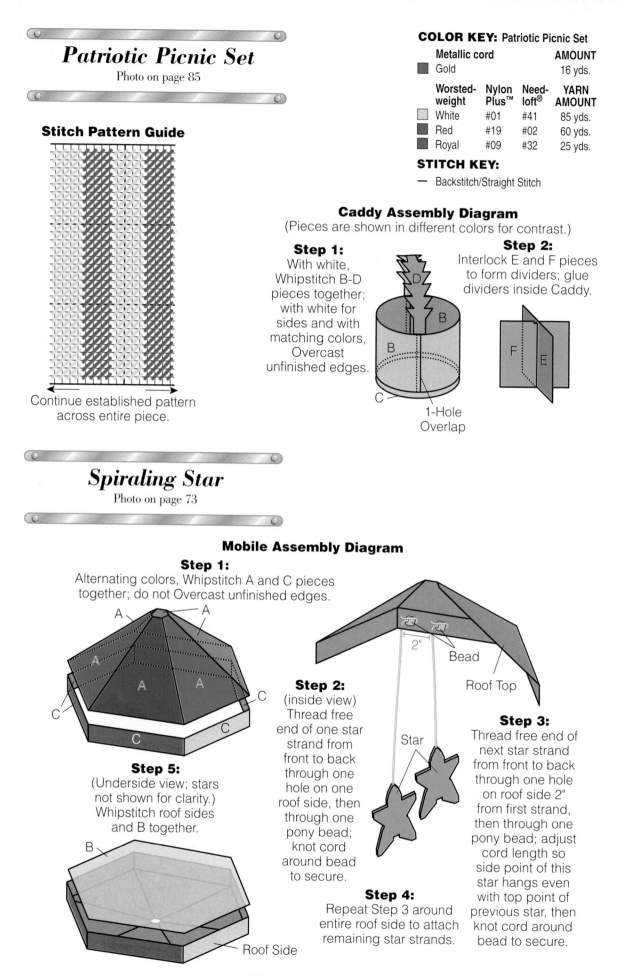

Continue established pattern across entire piece.

Caddy Assembly Diagram
(Pieces are shown in different colors for contrast.)

Step 1:
With white, Whipstitch B-D pieces together; with white for sides and with matching colors, Overcast unfinished edges.

Step 2:
Interlock E and F pieces to form dividers; glue dividers inside Caddy.

D

B

B

C

1-Hole Overlap

F

E

Spiraling Star

Photo on page 73

Mobile Assembly Diagram

Step 1:
Alternating colors, Whipstitch A and C pieces together; do not Overcast unfinished edges.

A

A

A

A

A

C

C

C

Step 5:
(Underside view; stars not shown for clarity.) Whipstitch roof sides and B together.

B

Roof Side

Step 2:
(inside view)
Thread free end of one star strand from front to back through one hole on one roof side, then through one pony bead; knot cord around bead to secure.

Star

Step 4:
Repeat Step 3 around entire roof side to attach remaining star strands.

2"

Bead

Roof Top

Step 3:
Thread free end of next star strand from front to back through one hole on roof side 2" from first strand, then through one pony bead; adjust cord length so side point of this star hangs even with top point of previous star, then knot cord around bead to secure.

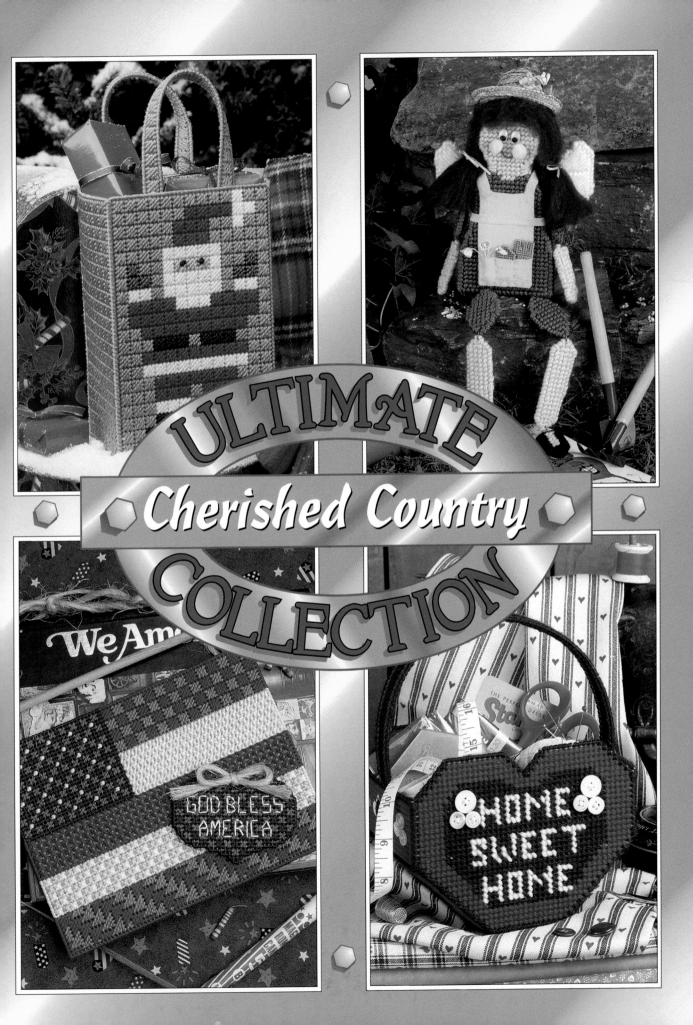

ULTIMATE

Cherished Country

COLLECTION

GOD BLESS
AMERICA

HOME
SWEET
HOME

Load up the sleigh with gifts and let this friendly St. Nick carry surprises galore.

Mosaic Santa Bag

Designed by Michele Wilcox

Size:
4" x 6⅛" x 9⅜",
not including handles.

Materials:
Two sheets of 7-count plastic canvas;
Craft glue or glue gun; Worsted-weight
or plastic canvas yarn (for amounts see
Color Key).

Stitching Instructions:

1: Using colors and stitches indicated, work
A-C pieces according to graph and stitch
pattern guide. Using gold and Scotch Stitch
over three bars, work D across length of
each piece; Overcast edges of handles.

2: Using black and French Knot, embroider
eyes on A pieces as indicated on graph.

3: With gold, Whipstitch A-C pieces together;
Overcast unfinished edges.

4: Glue handle ends to inside of bag as shown
in photo. ✧

Cutting Instructions:

A: For front and back, cut two (one for front
and one for back) 40 x 61 holes.

B: For sides, cut two 25 x 61 holes (no
graph).

C: For bottom, cut one 25 x 40 holes (no
graph).

D: For handles, cut two 4 x 70 holes (no
graph).

COLOR KEY: Mosaic Santa Bag

	Worsted-weight	Nylon Plus™	Need-loft®	YARN AMOUNT
	Gold	#27	#17	2½ oz.
	Dk. Red	#20	#01	18 yds.
	White	#01	#41	12 yds.
	Black	#02	#00	8 yds.
	Dk. Green	#31	#27	2 yds.
	Coral	–	#65	1 yd.

STITCH KEY:
● French Knot

Bag Stitch Pattern Guide

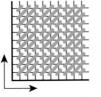

Continue established
pattern up and across
each entire piece.

A – Bag Front & Back
(cut 1 each) 40 x 61 holes

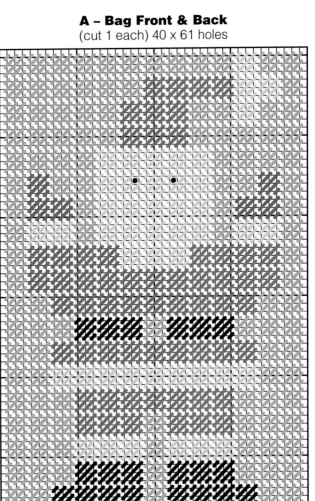

Remember childhood
days with a nostalgic toy
at home in any era.

My Little Wagon

Designed by Carol Nartowicz

Size:
5¾" x 7" x 6½" tall.

Materials:
Two sheets of 7-count plastic canvas; Craft glue or glue gun; Worsted-weight or plastic canvas yarn (for amounts see Color Key).

Cutting Instructions:
(**Note:** Graphs continued on page 94.)
A: For sides, cut two according to graph.
B: For ends, cut two according to graph.
C: For bottom, cut one according to graph.
D: For handle, cut one according to graph.
E: For wheel pieces, cut sixteen according to graph.

F: For lid base, cut one according to graph.
G: For lid, cut one 30 x 40 holes.
H: For lid handle, cut one 5 x 13 holes (no graph).

Stitching Instructions:
(**Note:** C, F and twelve E pieces are not worked.)
1: Using colors and stitches indicated, work A, B, D, four E and G pieces according to graphs. Using dk. red and Slanted Gobelin Stitch over narrow width, work H. With matching colors, Overcast cutout edges of A and B (omit indicated lid base attachment edges) pieces, G and long edges of H.
2: Whipstitch A-D and F pieces together as indicated on graphs and according to Wagon Assembly Diagram on page 94. For each wheel (make 4), holding three unworked E

pieces to wrong side of one worked piece, with black, Whipstitch together through all thicknesses. With dk. red, Whipstitch one short end of H to each indicated area on right side of G.

3: Glue wheels to sides and handle to end of Wagon as shown in photo. ✧

A – Side (cut 2) 25 x 42 holes

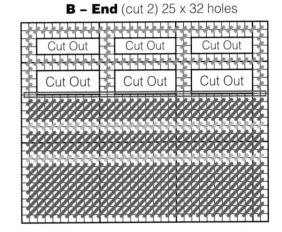

B – End (cut 2) 25 x 32 holes

COLOR KEY: My Little Wagon

	Worsted-weight	Nylon Plus™	Need-loft®	YARN AMOUNT
■ Dk. Red		#20	#01	23 yds.
Gold		#27	#17	14 yds.
■ Black		#02	#00	11 yds.
Cinnamon		#44	#14	10 yds.
White		#01	#41	7 yds.

STITCH KEY:

☐ Lid Base Attachment
☐ Lid Handle Attachment

E – Wheel Piece
(cut 16) 10 x 10 holes

C – Bottom (cut 2) 32 x 46 holes

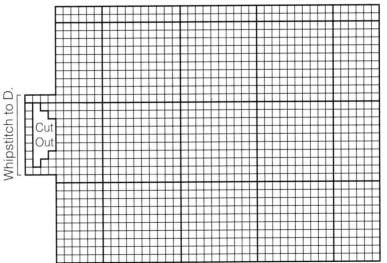

My Little Wagon

Photo on page 92

G – Lid (cut 1) 30 x 40 holes

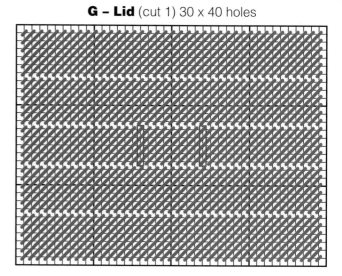

COLOR KEY: My Little Wagon

Worsted-weight	Nylon Plus™	Need-loft®	YARN AMOUNT
■ Dk. Red	#20	#01	23 yds.
■ Gold	#27	#17	14 yds.
■ Black	#02	#00	11 yds.
■ Cinnamon	#44	#14	10 yds.
■ White	#01	#41	7 yds.

STITCH KEY:
☐ Lid Base Attachment
☐ Lid Handle Attachment

F – Lid Base (cut 1) 32 x 42 holes

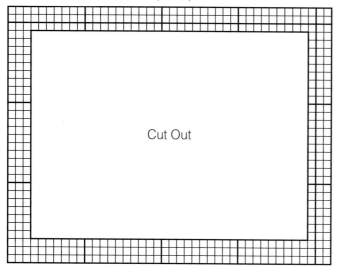

Cut Out

D – Handle
(cut 1) 12 x 42 holes

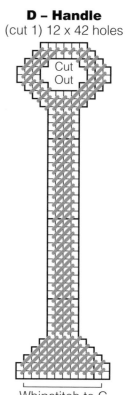

Cut Out

Whipstitch to C.

Wagon Assembly Diagram
(Some pieces are shown in different colors for contrast.)

Step 1:
With dk. red, Whipstitch F to indicated areas of A and B pieces.

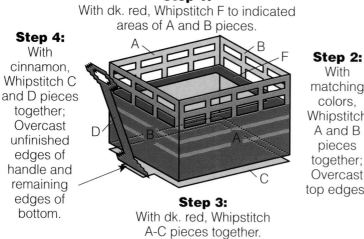

Step 4:
With cinnamon, Whipstitch C and D pieces together; Overcast unfinished edges of handle and remaining edges of bottom.

Step 2:
With matching colors, Whipstitch A and B pieces together; Overcast top edges.

Step 3:
With dk. red, Whipstitch A-C pieces together.

Country Flag Sampler

Designed by Raylene Hlavaty

Size:
Flag is 8⅜" x 11".

Materials:
One sheet of 7-count plastic canvas; 11" length of ⅜" wooden dowel; 3 yds. of bailer twine; Craft glue or glue gun; White wicking yarn or six-strand embroidery floss (for amount see Color Key on page 96); Worsted-weight or plastic canvas yarn (for amounts see Color Key).

Cutting Instructions:
(**Note:** Graphs on page 96.)
A: For flag, cut one 55 x 73 holes.
B: For heart, cut one according to graph.

Stitching Instructions:
1: Using colors and stitches indicated, work pieces according to graphs; with dk. royal for heart and with matching colors, Overcast edges.
2: Using wicking yarn or six strands floss and embroidery stitches indicated, embroider

CONTINUED ON PAGE 96

Country Flag Sampler

Continued from page 95

message on B as indicated on graph.

(**Note:** Cut one 2" and one 9" length of twine.)

3: Fold 9" length into bow loops, then wrap 2" length around center and glue ends at back to secure, forming bow. Glue bow to heart and heart to flag (see photo).

(**Note:** Cut two 6" lengths of twine.)

4: For each hanger loop, fold one 6" length in half and glue ends to back of flag at one top corner (see photo). Thread dowel through loops as shown in photo; glue to secure. Tie ends of remaining twine into a bow, forming hanger. Fold hanger in half with bow at center and twist together; glue hanger to ends of dowel as shown.✧

COLOR KEY: Country Flag Sampler

Wicking yarn or floss			AMOUNT
■ White			6 yds.

	Worsted-weight	Nylon Plus™	Need-loft®	YARN AMOUNT
■	Dk. Red	#20	#01	30 yds.
▨	Dusty Rose	#52	#06	28 yds.
▨	Dk. Royal	#07	#48	24 yds.
▨	White	#01	#41	23 yds.
▨	Beige	#43	#40	20 yds.
▨	Denim	#06	#33	16 yds.

STITCH KEY:

— Backstitch/Straight Stitch

B – Heart
(cut 1) 21 x 31 holes

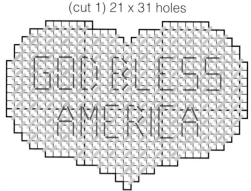

A – Flag
(cut 1) 55 x 73 holes

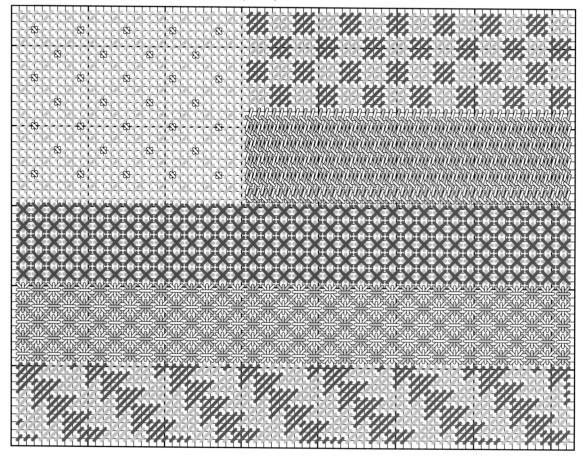

Baskets of Violets

Designed by Michele Wilcox

Size:
Each Coaster is 5" x 5¼";
Holder is 2¼" x 5¼" x
2½" tall.

Materials:
2½ sheets of 7-count plastic canvas; #3
pearl cotton or six-strand embroidery floss
(for amounts see Color Key); Worsted-
weight or plastic canvas yarn (for amounts
see Color Key).

Cutting Instructions:
(**Note:** Graphs continued
on page 102.)
(Note: Graphs continued on page 102.)
A: For Coasters, cut four
according to graph.
B: For Holder sides, cut
two 16 x 34 holes.
C: For Holder ends, cut
two 14 x 16 holes.
D: For Holder bottom, cut
one 14 x 34 holes (no
graph).

Stitching Instructions:
(**Note:** D piece is not
worked.)

1: Using colors indicated and Continental Stitch,
work A-C pieces according to graphs; fill in
uncoded areas using beige and Continental
Stitch. With matching colors, Overcast edges of
A pieces.
2: Using pearl cotton or six strands floss and
embroidery stitches indicated, embroider detail
on A pieces as indicated on graph.
3: With purple, Whipstitch B-D pieces together,
forming Holder; Overcast unfinished edges. ✧

COLOR KEY: Baskets of Violets

#3 pearl cotton or floss			AMOUNT
Lt. Purple			20 yds.
Teal			20 yds.
Navy			8 yds.
Tangerine			5 yds.

Worsted-weight	Nylon Plus™	Need-loft®	YARN AMOUNT
Beige	#43	#40	34 yds.
Purple	#21	#46	28 yds.
Sea Green	#37	#53	24 yds.
Dusty Blue	#38	#34	16 yds.
Black	#02	#00	8 yds.
Dk. Orange	#18	#52	3 yds.

STITCH KEY:
— Backstitch/Straight Stitch

A – Coaster
(cut 4) 32 x 34 holes
Cut out gray areas carefully.

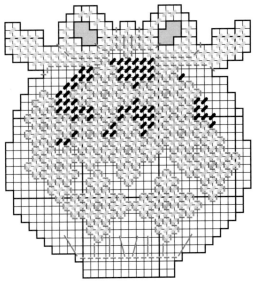

Home Sweet Home

Designed by Tamara Will

Size:
4½" x 6¾" x 9" tall, including handle.

Materials:
Two sheets of 7-count plastic canvas; 24 assorted sizes of off-white buttons; 2 yds. white six-strand embroidery floss; Sewing needle; Two 9" x 12" sheets of coordinating-color felt (optional); Craft glue or glue gun; Worsted-weight or plastic canvas yarn (for amounts see Color Key).

Cutting Instructions:
A: For sides, cut two according to graph.
B: For end tops, cut two 12 x 29 holes.
C: For end bottoms, cut two 20 x 29 holes.
D: For bottom, cut one 15 x 29 holes (no graph).
E: For handle, cut one 6 x 90 holes (no graph).

Stitching Instructions:
(**Note:** D piece is not worked.)
1: Using colors and stitches indicated, work A–C and E pieces according to graphs and stitch pattern guide; with dk. royal, Overcast edges of E.

2: Using sewing needle and six strands floss, sew six buttons to each side and end top as desired (see photo).

3: With dk. royal, Whipstitch A-D pieces together as indicated on graphs and according to Basket Assembly Diagram; Overcast unfinished edges.

4: If desired, line inside of Basket with felt. Glue handle ends inside Basket at ends (see photo).✧

COLOR KEY: Home Sweet Home

	Worsted-weight	Nylon Plus™	Need-loft®	YARN AMOUNT
■	Crimson	#53	#42	28 yds.
■	Dk. Royal	#07	#48	20 yds.
■	Eggshell	#24	#39	10 yds.

A – Side (cut 2) 32 x 43 holes

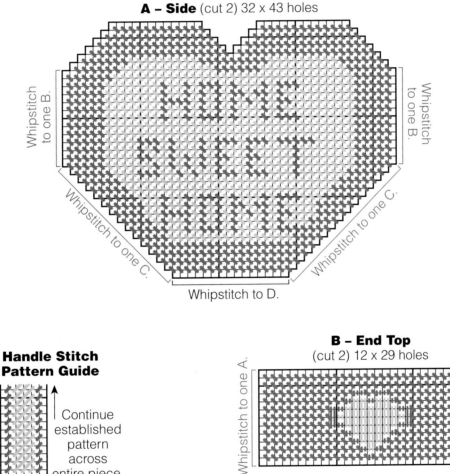

Whipstitch to one B.

Whipstitch to one B.

Whipstitch to one C.

Whipstitch to one C.

Whipstitch to D.

Handle Stitch Pattern Guide

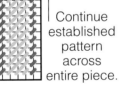

Continue established pattern across entire piece.

Basket Assembly Diagram

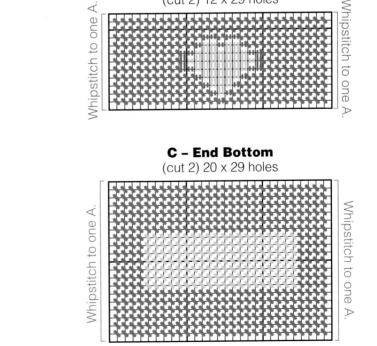

B – End Top
(cut 2) 12 x 29 holes

Whipstitch to one A.

Whipstitch to one A.

C – End Bottom
(cut 2) 20 x 29 holes

Whipstitch to one A.

Whipstitch to one A.

Garden Angel
Photo on page 100

Arm & Sleeve Assembly Diagram
Step 1: Thread ends of one wire from front to back through ✦ hole on arm and one ✦ hole on sleeve; twist ends together to secure.

Step 2: Thread second wire from front to back through opposite ✦ hole on sleeve and through yarn at ✦ hole on body side; twist ends together to secure.

Body Side
Sleeve
Wire
Arm

Leg & Foot Assembly Diagram
Step 1: Thread ends of one wire from front to back through ✦ hole on body front and one ✦ hole on upper leg; twist ends together to secure.

Step 2: Thread second wire from front to back through opposite ✦ hole on upper leg and through one ✦ hole on lower leg; twist ends together to secure.

Body Front
Upper Leg
Wire
Lower Leg
Wire
Foot

Step 3: Thread third wire from front to back through opposite ✦ hole on lower leg and through ✦ hole on foot; twist ends together to secure.

K – Apron & Apron Pocket Cutting Guide
KEY:
— Cutting Line

3/8" 3/8"

Scrap

Apron Pocket

1"
2"
3³/₄"
7"

Apron

2"

Body Assembly Diagram

B
A
B
A
C

Apron Assembly Diagram

Apron
Apron Pocket
5/8" 3/4" 5/8"

KEY:
···· Sewing Line

Basket of Violets
Photo on page 97

C – Holder End
(cut 2) 14 x 16 holes

B – Holder Side
(cut 2) 16 x 34 holes

COLOR KEY: Baskets of Violets

#3 pearl cotton or floss			AMOUNT
Lt. Purple			20 yds.
Teal			20 yds.
Navy			8 yds.
Tangerine			5 yds.

Worsted-weight	Nylon Plus™	Need-loft®	YARN AMOUNT
Beige	#43	#40	34 yds.
Purple	#21	#46	28 yds.
Sea Green	#37	#53	24 yds.
Dusty Blue	#38	#34	16 yds.
Black	#02	#00	8 yds.
Dk. Orange	#18	#52	3 yds.

STITCH KEY:
— Backstitch/Straight Stitch

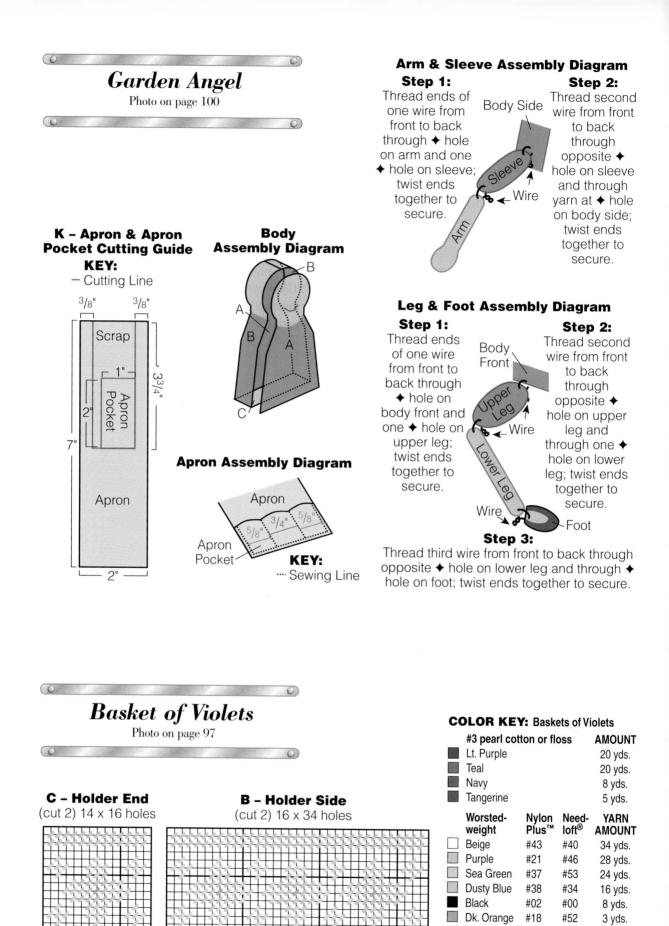

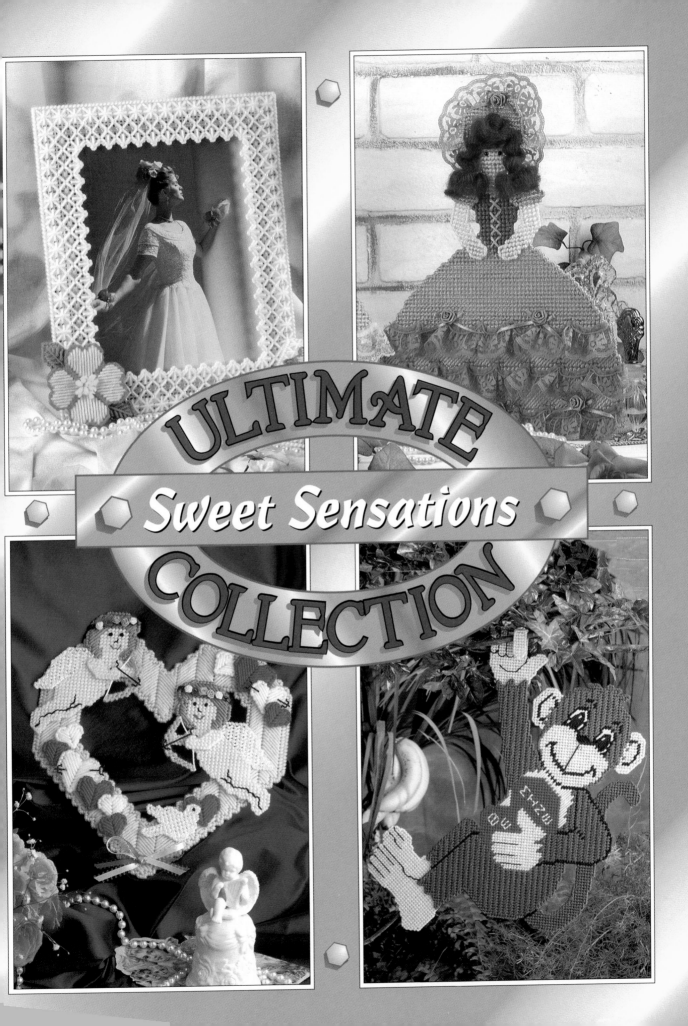

ULTIMATE

Sweet Sensations

COLLECTION

Southern Belles

Designed by
Robin Howard Will

Size:
Tissue Box Cover is 4¾" x 9½" x about 13½" tall and snugly covers a 3" x 4½" x 9¼" long tissue box; Window Screen is 13½" x 38" when flat.

Materials:
11 sheets of 7-count plastic canvas; 10 black 4-mm half-round beads; Six each blue, mauve, yellow, lt. green and lilac ½" satin ribbon roses; 1½ yds. each blue, mauve, yellow, lt. green and lilac ⅛" satin ribbon; 2⅔ yds. blue and 1¼ yds. each mauve, yellow, lt.

green and lilac 1" pregathered lace; Auburn wool doll hair; Craft glue or glue gun; Worsted-weight or plastic canvas yarn (for amounts see Color Key on page 117).

Cutting Instructions:
(**Note:** Graphs on pages 116-118.)
A: For Belles and backings, cut nine (five for Belles and four for backings) according to graph.
B: For Tissue Cover Belle backing, cut one according to graph.
C: For arms #1 and #2, cut five each according to graphs.
D: For bonnets, cut five according to graph.
E: For Tissue Cover top, cut one according to

graph.

F: For Tissue Cover back, cut one 21 x 62 holes.

G: For Tissue Cover ends #1 and #2, cut one each according to graphs.

Stitching Instructions:
(**Note:** Four A pieces are not worked for backings.)

1: For Tissue Cover Belle, using colors and stitches indicated, work one A, B, one of each C, one D and E-G pieces according to graphs; with sail blue, Overcast cutout edges of E.

2: Using colors and embroidery stitches indicated, embroider mouth and bodice ties as indicated on A graph.

3: With sail blue, Whipstitch X edges of D

right sides together as indicated; with matching colors, Overcast edges of C and D pieces.

4: With sail blue, Whipstitch A, B and E-G pieces together as indicated and according to Tissue Cover Assembly Diagram on page 117.

(**Note:** Cut blue lace into one 9", one 12" and two 36" lengths.)

5: Glue 9" lace around back outer edges of bonnet. Using Cross Stitches as a guide for scallop points, glue 12" lace in a scallop pattern across top row on front of skirt. Using one 36" lace for each remaining row of Cross Stitches, glue lace in a scallop pattern around entire Cover.

CONTINUED ON PAGE 116

Cherish memories of that special day with a lacy photo frame and trinket box pair.

Bridal Keepsakes

Designed by Kimberly Suber

Size:
Frame is 10" x 11¾" and has a 6½" x 8¼" photo window; Box is 4" x 4½" x 2⅛" tall, not including flower.

Materials:
Three sheets of 7-count plastic canvas; 92 white 4-mm pearls; Sewing needle and white thread; Craft glue or glue gun; ⅛" satin ribbon (for amount see Color Key); Worsted-weight or plastic canvas yarn (for amounts see Color Key).

Cutting Instructions:
(**Note:** Graphs continued on pages 108 & 109.)

A: For Frame front, cut one according to graph.

B: For Frame back, cut one according to graph.

C: For Frame stand, cut one 27 x 51 holes (no graph).

D: For lid top, cut one 25 x 29 holes.

E: For lid long and short sides, cut two each according to graphs.

F: For box long and short sides, cut two 13 x 27 holes for long sides and two 13 x 23 holes for short sides.

G: For box bottom, cut one 23 x 27 holes (no graph).

H: For flower petals, cut eight according to graph.

I: For leaves, cut four according to graph.

Stitching Instructions:
(**Note:** B, C and G pieces are not worked.)

1: Using ribbon and yarn colors and stitches indicated, work A, D-F, H and I pieces according to graphs; with white, Overcast cutout edges of A. With green, Overcast I pieces.

2: With thread, sew beads to A and E pieces as indicated on graphs.

3: For Frame, with white, Whipstitch one short end of C to B as indicated; holding A and B pieces wrong sides together, Whipstitch together.

4: With white, Whipstitch D and E pieces together, forming lid; Whipstitch F and G pieces together, forming box. Overcast edges of lid and box.

5: For each flower, with watermelon, Whipstitch four H pieces together as indicated and according to Flower Assembly Diagram; Overcast edges. Using yellow and Modified Turkey Work (make ⅜" loops), embroider flower center on each H piece as indicated; clip through loops and fray ends slightly.

6: Glue two leaves and one flower to Frame and remaining leaves and flower to lid as shown in photo. ✧

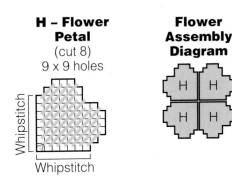

H – Flower Petal
(cut 8)
9 x 9 holes

Whipstitch

Whipstitch

Flower Assembly Diagram

I – Leaf
(cut 4)
7 x 7 holes

COLOR KEY: Bridal Keepsakes

⅛" satin ribbon			AMOUNT
■ Pink			3½ yds.

	Worsted-weight	Nylon Plus™	Need-loft®	YARN AMOUNT
▨	White	#01	#41	42 yds.
	Pink	#11	#07	8 yds.
□	Watermelon	#54	#55	4 yds.
■	Green	#58	#28	3 yds.
	Yellow	#26	#57	2 yds.

STITCH KEY:
▲ Modified Turkey Work
○ Pearl Attachment
☐ Stand Attachment

Bridal Keepsakes
Photo on page 106

COLOR KEY: Bridal Keepsakes

1/8" satin ribbon			AMOUNT
■ Pink			3 1/2 yds.

Worsted-weight	Nylon Plus™	Need-loft®	YARN AMOUNT
▨ White	#01	#41	42 yds.
▨ Pink	#11	#07	8 yds.
□ Watermelon	#54	#55	4 yds.
■ Green	#58	#28	3 yds.
▨ Yellow	#26	#57	2 yds.

STITCH KEY:
- ▲ Modified Turkey Work
- ○ Pearl Attachment
- □ Stand Attachment

A – Frame Front (cut 1) 65 x 77 holes

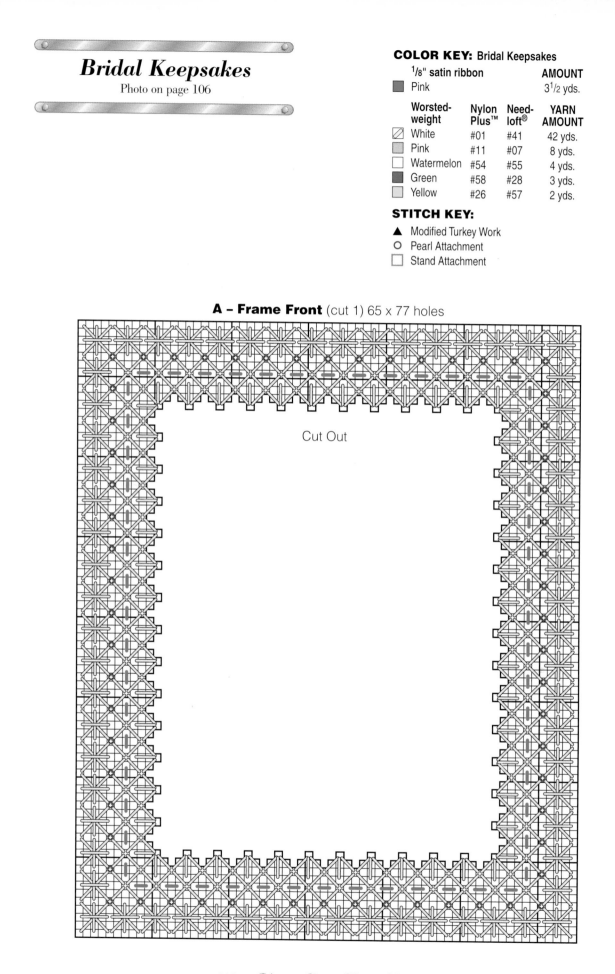

Cut Out

B – Frame Back (cut 1) 65 x 77 holes

Opposite end is 77 holes from top edge.

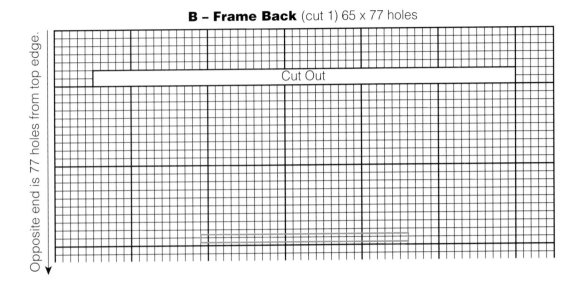

Cut Out

D – Lid Top (cut 1) 25 x 29 holes

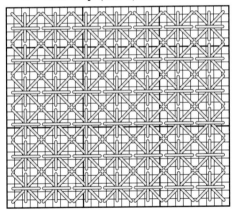

E – Lid Long Side
(cut 2) 5 x 29 holes

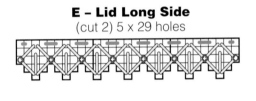

E – Lid Short Side
(cut 2) 5 x 25 holes

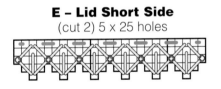

F – Box Long Side
(cut 2) 13 x 27 holes

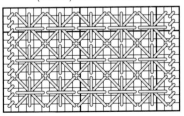

F – Box Short Side
(cut 2) 13 x 23 holes

Be Mine Monkey

Designed by Diane T. Ray

Size:
14½" x 16½".

Materials:
One 12" x 18" or larger sheet of 7-count plastic canvas; One Velcro® closure; Craft glue or glue gun; Worsted-weight or plastic canvas yarn (for amounts see Color Key).

Cutting Instructions:

A: For body, cut one according to graph on page 112.

B: For feet, cut one according to graph.

C: For hand, cut one according to graph.

D: For knuckle, cut one 3 x 4 holes.

E: For finger, cut one according to graph.

Stitching Instructions:

1: Using colors and stitches indicated, work pieces according to graphs; with beige, Whipstitch C-E pieces together according to Hand Assembly Diagram on page 112.

2: With black for back elbow, maple for face and with matching colors as shown in photo, Overcast edges of A and B pieces and hand.

(**Note:** Separate remaining black and white into 2-ply or nylon plastic canvas yarn into 1-ply strands.)

3: Using 2-ply (or 1-ply) in colors and embroidery stitches indicated, embroider letters and detail as indicated on graphs.

4: Cut closure to match shape of fingertip; glue loopy side of closure to C as indicated and fuzzy side to underside of fingertip.

5: Glue feet and hand to back of A as shown in photo.✧

B – Feet
(cut 1)
28 x 34 holes

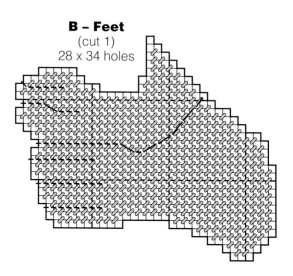

COLOR KEY: Be Mine Monkey

	Worsted-weight	Nylon Plus™	Need-loft®	YARN AMOUNT
▨	Maple	#35	#13	35 yds.
▨	Beige	#43	#40	24 yds.
▨	Dk. Red	#20	#01	7 yds.
■	Black	#02	#00	6 yds.
▨	Dk. Brown	#36	#15	1 yd.
▨	White	#01	#41	1 yd.

STITCH KEY:

— Backstitch/Straight Stitch
☐ Closure Attachment

D – Knuckle
(cut 1)
3 x 4 holes
Whipstitch to C.

Whipstitch to E.

E – Finger
(cut 1)
4 x 9 holes
Whipstitch to D.

Whipstitch to D.

C – Hand
(cut 1)
21 x 22 holes

*Swing into the heart
of someone you love
with a scampy monkey Valentine.*

Be Mine Monkey
Photo on page 111

COLOR KEY: Be Mine Monkey

Worsted-weight	Nylon Plus™	Need-loft®	YARN AMOUNT
Maple	#35	#13	35 yds.
Beige	#43	#40	24 yds.
Dk. Red	#20	#01	7 yds.
Black	#02	#00	6 yds.
Dk. Brown	#36	#15	1 yd.
White	#01	#41	1 yd.

STITCH KEY:

— Backstitch/Straight Stitch
☐ Closure Attachment

Hand Assembly Diagram

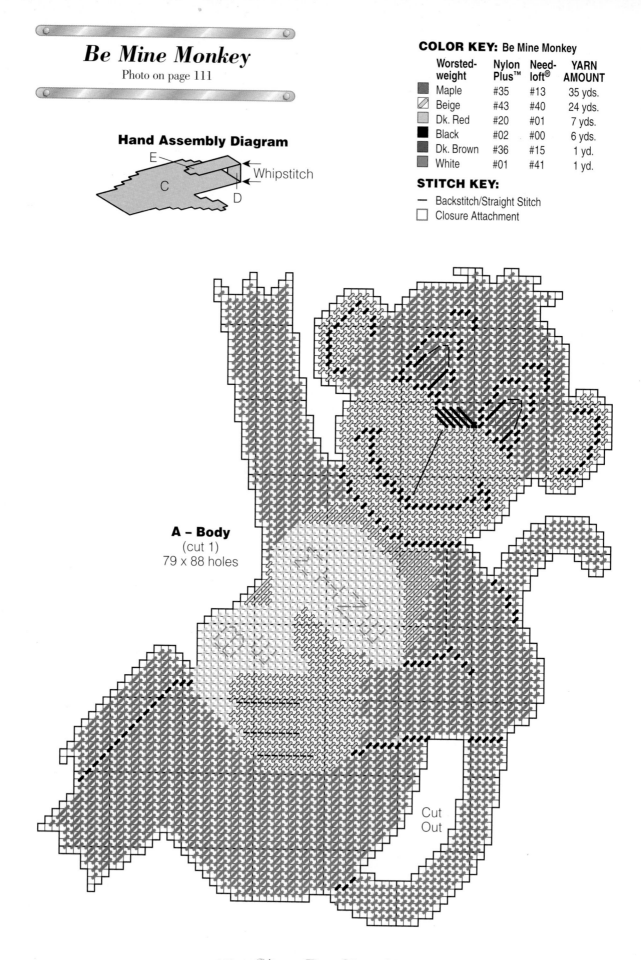

A – Body
(cut 1)
79 x 88 holes

Valentine Wreath

Designed by Robin Petrina

Instructions on page 114

Spark a flame of romance when these winsome cupids draw back their bows.

Valentine Wreath

Photo on page 113

Size:
10⅝" x 11½".

Materials:
Three sheets of 7-count plastic canvas; Scraps of black and white 7-count plastic canvas; ¼ yd. each of white and rose ¼" picot-edged satin ribbon; 10 assorted-color small ribbon roses; 1 yd. brown raffia straw; ¾" plastic ring; Craft glue or glue gun; Pearlized metallic cord (for amount see Color Key); Worsted-weight or plastic canvas yarn (for amounts see Color Key).

Cutting Instructions:
(**Note:** Use white for D, black for E and clear canvas for remaining pieces.)

A: For Wreath front and backing, cut two (one for front and one for backing) according to graph.

B: For cherubs #1 and #2, cut one each according to graphs.

C: For arms #1 and #2, cut one each according to graphs.

D: For bow, cut two according to graph.

E: For arrows #1 and #2, cut number indicated according to graphs.

F: For large hearts, cut two according to graph.

G: For medium hearts, cut three according to graph.

H: For small hearts, cut six according to graph.

I: For dove, cut one according to graph.

Stitching Instructions:
(**Note:** Backing A is not worked.)

1: Using colors and stitches indicated, work one A for front, B, C, one F, two G, three H and I pieces according to graphs; substituting white for crimson, work remaining F-H

pieces according to graphs. With matching colors, Overcast edges of B, C and F-I pieces. Omitting single straight bar, with pewter, Overcast edges of D pieces.

2: With white, sew ring to center top of backing A. Holding A pieces wrong sides together, with pink, Whipstitch together, forming wreath.

3: Using colors (separate yarn, if desired) and embroidery stitches indicated, embroider detail on B and I pieces as indicated on graphs.

(**Note:** Cut raffia into three equal lengths; braid strands together.)

4: Cut raffia braid in half, and glue one braid around head of each cherub as shown in photo; glue five roses to center of each braid.

5: Holding ribbons together, tie into a bow; trim ends. Glue one E#1 to each D and one bow and corresponding arm to each cherub as shown. Glue cherubs, hearts and dove to wreath as shown. Glue E#2 pieces to hearts as desired or as shown. ✧

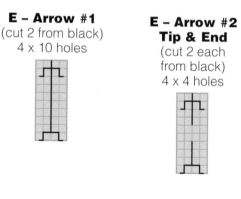

E – Arrow #1
(cut 2 from black)
4 x 10 holes

E – Arrow #2
Tip & End
(cut 2 each from black)
4 x 4 holes

COLOR KEY: Valentine Wreath

	Pearlized cord			AMOUNT
▨	White			7 yds.

	Worsted-weight	Nylon Plus™	Need-loft®	YARN AMOUNT
	Pink	#11	#07	22 yds.
	Flesh	#14	#56	13 yds.
	Crimson	#53	#42	8 yds.
	White	#01	#41	7 yds.
	Camel	#34	#43	5 yds.
	Pewter	#40	#65	2 yds.
	Black	#02	#00	1½ yds.
	Red	#19	#02	½ yd.

STITCH KEY:
— Backstitch/Straight Stitch
● French Knot

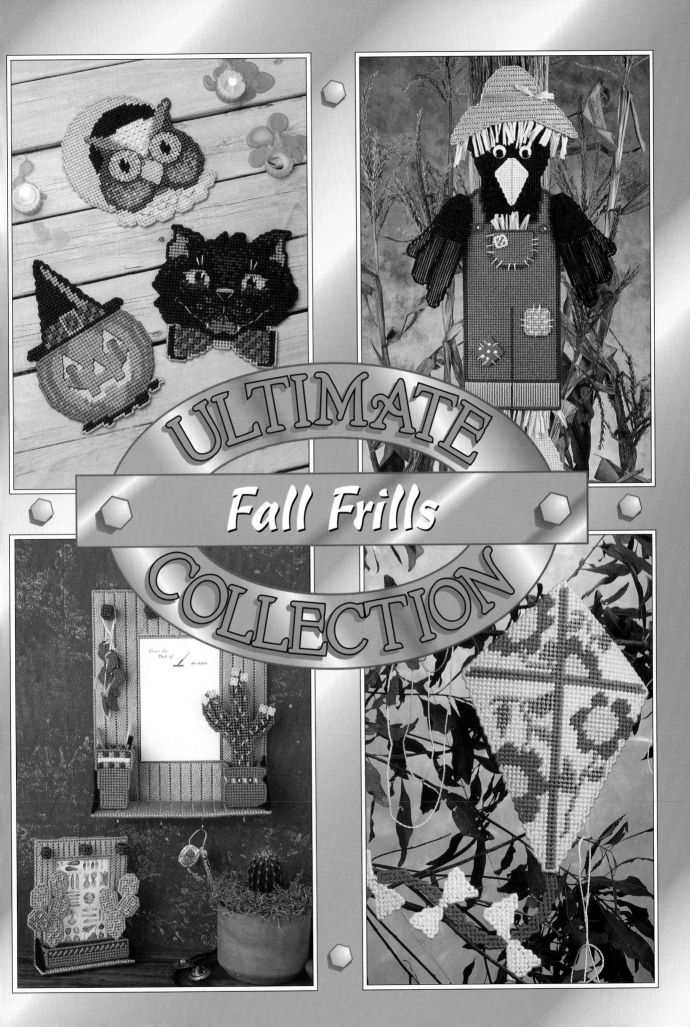

ULTIMATE

Fall Frills

COLLECTION

Halloween Faces

Designed by Janelle Giese of Janelle Marie Designs

Size:
Pumpkin is 5⅝" x 8¾";
Owl is 7" x 7"; Cat is 6½" x 7¼".

Materials:
1½ sheets of 7-count plastic canvas; ⅛"
metallic ribbon or metallic cord (for
amount see individual Color Keys; Owl and
Cat keys on page 122); Six-strand embroidery
floss (for amounts see individual Color Keys);
Worsted-weight or plastic canvas yarn (for
amounts see individual Color Keys.)

Cutting Instructions:
A: For Pumpkin, cut one according to graph.
B: For Owl, cut one according to graph on
page 122.

C: For Cat, cut one according to graph on
page 122.

Stitching Instructions:
1: Using colors and stitches indicated, work
pieces according to graphs; fill in uncoded
areas using black and Continental Stitch.
With ribbon or cord for Pumpkin's collar,
Owl's moon and Cat's bow and with matching colors as shown in photo, Overcast
edges.
2: Using four strands floss, yarn and ribbon or
cord in colors and embroidery stitches indicated, embroider detail as indicated on
graphs.
3: Hang as desired. ✧

COLOR KEY: Pumpkin

	Embroidery floss			AMOUNT
■	Dk. Brown			2 yds.

	⅛" metallic ribbon or cord			AMOUNT
▧	Gold			2 yds.

	Worsted-weight	Nylon Plus™	Need-loft®	YARN AMOUNT
▨	Dk. Rust	#16	#10	9 yds.
▨	Pumpkin	#50	#12	9 yds.
☐	Black	#02	#00	7 yds.
▧	Yellow	#26	#57	4 yds.
▨	Gray	#23	#38	2 yds.
▨	Green	#58	#28	2 yds.
■	Purple	#21	#46	2 yds.

STITCH KEY:
— Backstitch/Straight Stitch

A – Pumpkin
(cut 1)
37 x 57 holes

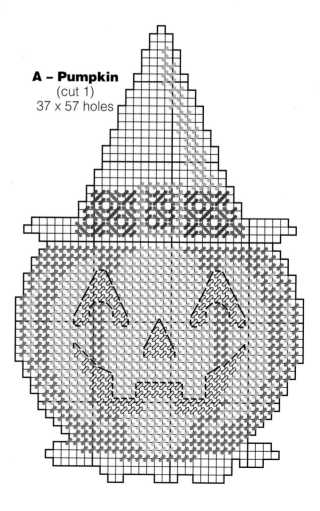

*Invite these
creatures of the night
to your next
Halloween bash.*

Halloween Faces

Photo on page 121

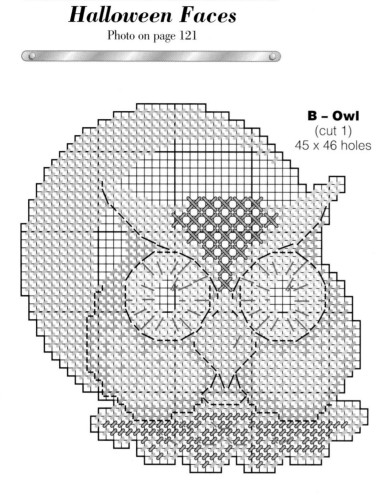

B – Owl
(cut 1)
45 x 46 holes

COLOR KEY: Owl

Embroidery floss			AMOUNT
■ Dk. Brown			3 yds.
▨ Ecru			2 yds.
▨ Camel			1 yd.

1/8" metallic ribbon or cord			AMOUNT
▢ Gold			5 yds.

Worsted-weight	Nylon Plus™	Need-loft®	YARN AMOUNT
▨ Beige	#43	#40	10 yds.
▨ Camel	#34	#43	5 yds.
▨ Cinnamon	#44	#14	5 yds.
▢ Black	#02	#00	4 yds.
▨ Eggshell	#24	#39	3 yds.

STITCH KEY:

— Backstitch/Straight Stitch

COLOR KEY: Cat

Embroidery floss			AMOUNT
▨ Gray			2 yds.
▨ Ecru			1 yd.

1/8" metallic ribbon or cord			AMOUNT
▢ Gold			3 yds.

Worsted-weight	Nylon Plus™	Need-loft®	YARN AMOUNT
■ Black	#02	#00	22 yds.
▨ Dk. Royal	#07	#48	4 yds.
▨ Camel	#34	#43	2 yds.
▨ Green	#58	#28	2 yds.
▨ Purple	#21	#46	2 yds.
▨ Beige	#43	#40	1 yd.
▨ Gray	#23	#38	1 yd.
▨ Dusty Rose	#52	#06	1 yd.

STITCH KEY:

— Backstitch/Straight Stitch

C – Cat
(cut 1) 44 x 47 holes

Cat Candy Wizard

Designed by Trudy Bath Smith

Size:
5¼" x 10¾" x 9¼" tall.

Materials:
Two sheets of 7-count plastic canvas;
Two blue 12-mm cat eyes (Cut off
shanks and file nubs smooth); Craft glue or
glue gun; Metallic cord (for amount see Color
Key on page 125); Worsted-weight or plastic
canvas yarn (for amounts see Color Key).

Cutting Instructions:
(**Note:** Graphs on pages 124 & 125.)
A: For base pieces, cut two according to
graph.
B: For cat head front and back, cut two (one for
front and one for back) according to graph.
C: For cat nose, cut one according to graph.
D: For cat body front and back, cut two (one
for front and one for back) according to
graph.
E: For cat arms, cut two according to graph.
F: For cat tail, cut one according to graph.

CONTINUED ON PAGE 124

Cat Candy Wizard

Continued from page 123

G: For moon, cut one according to graph.

H: For stars, cut three according to graph.

I: For hat top pieces, cut two according to graph.

J: For hat brim, cut one according to graph.

K: For pumpkin top, cut one according to graph.

L: For pumpkin front, cut one according to graph.

M: For pumpkin back, cut one according to graph.

N: For bowl, cut one 16 x 73 holes (no graph).

A – Base Piece
(cut 2) 33 x 70 holes

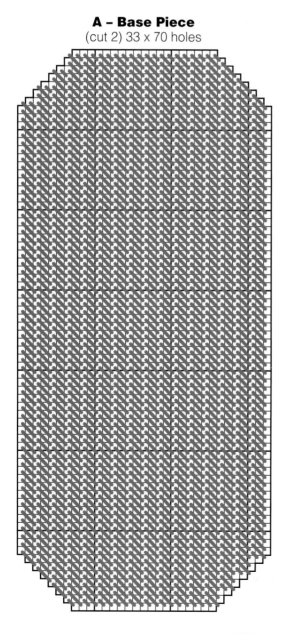

Stitching Instructions:

(**Note:** One A piece is not worked.)

1: Using colors and stitches indicated and leaving uncoded areas of M unworked, work one A, one B for front, C-M (one D and one E on opposite side of canvas) pieces according to graphs; using black and Continental Stitch, work remaining B for back.

2: With matching colors, Overcast edges of C (Whipstitch Y edges together as indicated on graph as you work), E-H, J and K pieces. With black, Overcast cutout edges of L.

3: Overlapping three holes at ends and working through both thicknesses at overlap area to join, using dk. orange and Slanted Gobelin Stitch over three bars, work N in vertical rows around entire piece.

4: Using colors and embroidery stitches indicated, embroider detail on D and I pieces as indicated.

5: For base, holding unworked A to wrong side of worked piece, with green, Whipstitch together. For head, holding B pieces wrong sides together, Whipstitch together as indicated; Overcast unfinished edges. For body, holding D pieces wrong sides together, with matching colors, Whipstitch together as indicated; omitting top edges, with black, Overcast unfinished edges.

6: For hat top, holding I pieces wrong sides together, Whipstitch together as indicated; with yellow, Overcast unfinished edges. For pumpkin, holding right side of M to wrong side of L, with dk. orange, Whipstitch together.

7: Glue C and cat eyes to front B as shown in photo; slip bottom opening of head over neck edges of body and glue to secure. Glue E and F pieces to body as indicated and as shown. Glue bottom edges of hat top to right side center of J, pumpkin to bowl and cat, hat, bowl and pumpkin to base; glue K to pumpkin as shown.

(**Note:** Cut one 3" and three 2" lengths of gold cord.)

8: Thread one 2" strand of cord through stitches on hand area of back arm; pull ends to even. Glue ends to back of G at top. Glue one end of each remaining strand to back of each H; glue opposite ends of cord to back of G at bottom (see photo). ✧

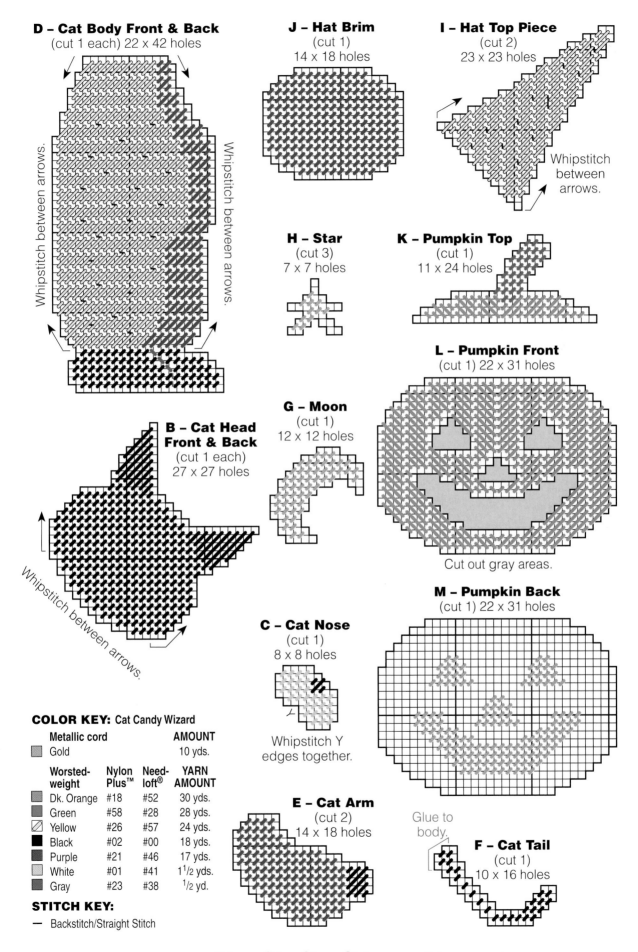

D – Cat Body Front & Back
(cut 1 each) 22 x 42 holes

Whipstitch between arrows.

Whipstitch between arrows.

J – Hat Brim
(cut 1)
14 x 18 holes

I – Hat Top Piece
(cut 2)
23 x 23 holes

Whipstitch between arrows.

H – Star
(cut 3)
7 x 7 holes

K – Pumpkin Top
(cut 1)
11 x 24 holes

L – Pumpkin Front
(cut 1) 22 x 31 holes

Cut out gray areas.

G – Moon
(cut 1)
12 x 12 holes

**B – Cat Head
Front & Back**
(cut 1 each)
27 x 27 holes

Whipstitch between arrows.

M – Pumpkin Back
(cut 1) 22 x 31 holes

C – Cat Nose
(cut 1)
8 x 8 holes

Whipstitch Y
edges together.

COLOR KEY: Cat Candy Wizard

	Metallic cord			AMOUNT
	Gold			10 yds.

	Worsted-weight	Nylon Plus™	Need-loft®	YARN AMOUNT
	Dk. Orange	#18	#52	30 yds.
	Green	#58	#28	28 yds.
	Yellow	#26	#57	24 yds.
	Black	#02	#00	18 yds.
	Purple	#21	#46	17 yds.
	White	#01	#41	1½ yds.
	Gray	#23	#38	½ yd.

STITCH KEY:
— Backstitch/Straight Stitch

E – Cat Arm
(cut 2)
14 x 18 holes

Glue to body.

F – Cat Tail
(cut 1)
10 x 16 holes

Autumn Breezes

Designed by Michele Wilcox

Size:
Kite is 7" x 9⅞";
Tail is 5" x 9⅝".

Materials:
One sheet of 7-count plastic canvas;
Worsted-weight or plastic canvas yarn
(for amounts see Color Key).

Cutting Instructions:
A: For kite, cut one according to graph.
B: For tail, cut one according to graph.

Stitching Instructions:
1: Using colors indicated and Continental
Stitch, work pieces according to graphs; with
matching colors, Overcast edges.
2: Hang or display as desired. ✧

A – Kite
(cut 1)
45 x 65 holes

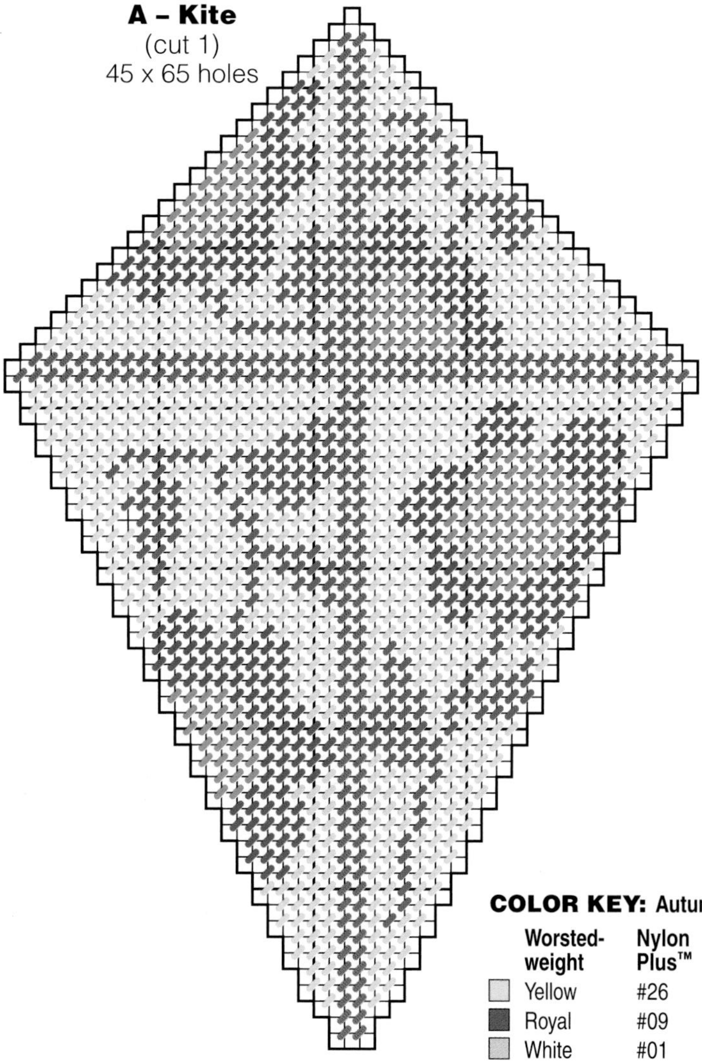

B – Tail
(cut 1)
29 x 63 holes

COLOR KEY: Autumn Breezes

	Worsted-weight	Nylon Plus™	Need-loft®	YARN AMOUNT
	Yellow	#26	#57	17 yds.
	Royal	#09	#32	15 yds.
	White	#01	#41	7 yds.
	Dk. Rust	#16	#10	6 yds.
	Sea Green	#37	#53	4 yds.
	Tangerine	#15	#11	3 yds.

Drift across country meadows when you launch a colorful kite banner.

Scary-Crow

Designed by Jacquelyn Fox

Size:
13⅜" x 26½".

Materials:
Two sheets of 12" x 18" or larger 7-count plastic canvas; Two 20-mm wiggle eyes; Two plaid ⅝" 4-hole buttons; Sewing needle; 6 yds. natural raffia straw; Craft glue or glue gun; Six-strand embroidery floss (for amount see Color Key on page 137); Worsted-weight or plastic canvas yarn (for amounts see Color Key).

Cutting Instructions:
(**Note:** Graphs on pages 137 & 138.)

A: For head and body, cut one according to graph.

B: For wings, cut two according to graph.

C: For feet, cut two according to graph.

D: For hat front, cut one according to graph.

E: For hat back, cut one according to graph.

F: For beak, cut one according to graph.

G: For pocket, cut one according to graph.

H: For large patch, cut one according to graph.

I: For medium patch, cut one 8 x 8 holes.

J: For small patch, cut one 4 x 4 holes.

Stitching Instructions:
1: Leaving uncoded area of E unworked, using colors and stitches indicated, work pieces (one B and one C on opposite side of canvas) according to graphs; with denim for G and overalls on A and with matching colors as shown in photo, Overcast edges.

2: Using camel and Backstitch, embroider

CONTINUED ON PAGE 137

Southwestern Windows

Designed by Vicki Blizzard

From the
Desk of . . .

Jan Jaynes

Instructions on page 132

Spooky Screen

Designed by Robin Petrina

Size:
6⅜" x 32" opened flat.

Materials:
2½ sheets of 7-count plastic canvas; Craft glue or glue gun; Worsted-weight or plastic canvas yarn (for amounts see Color Key).

Cutting Instructions:
A: For ghost panels, cut three 42 x 42 holes.
B: For jack-o-lantern panels, cut two 42 x 42 holes

Stitching Instructions:
1: Using colors and stitches indicated, work pieces according to graphs; fill in uncoded areas using black and Continental Stitch.

2: Using black and embroidery stitches indicated, embroider detail as indicated on graphs.

3: Alternating motifs, with purple, Whipstitch side edges of pieces together (see photo); Overcast unfinished edges.
(**Note:** Cut three 9" lengths of dk. orange.)

4: Tie each dk. orange strand into a small bow and trim ends; glue one bow to each ghost neck as shown. ✧

COLOR KEY: Spooky Screen

	Worsted-weight	Nylon Plus™	Need-loft®	YARN AMOUNT
■	Black	#02	#00	26 yds.
	Sand	#47	#16	18 yds.
	White	#01	#41	14 yds.
	Dk. Orange	#18	#52	13 yds.
	Silver	#40	#37	10 yds.
□	Purple	#21	#46	7 yds.
	Yellow	#26	#57	6 yds.
	Dk. Green	#31	#27	1 yd.

STITCH KEY:
— Backstitch/Straight Stitch
● French Knot

A – Ghost Panel
(cut 3) 42 x 42 holes

B – Jack-o-Lantern Panel
(cut 2) 42 x 42 holes

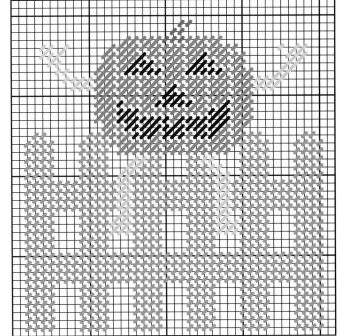

Southwestern Windows

Photo on page 129

Size:

Message Center is 2⅝" x 10⅛" x 12" with a 4½" x 6⅝" window that holds a 4" x 6" bottom-opening note pad; Frame is 4" x 5½" x 6¾" tall with a 3" x 4½" photo window.

Materials:

Three sheets of beige and four sheets of clear 7-count plastic canvas; Four gold cup hooks; 78 cream 6-mm bugle beads; One small note pad (see Size above); 2 yds. tan six-strand embroidery floss; 1½" sawtooth hanger; Sewing needle and white thread; Craft glue or glue gun; #3 pearl cotton or six-strand embroidery floss (for amount see Color Key on page 135); Worsted-weight or plastic canvas yarn (for amounts see Color Key).

Message Center

Cutting Instructions:

(**Notes:** Graphs on pages 134 & 135. Use beige for A and clear canvas for remaining pieces.)

A: For frame front and back, cut one each according to graph.

B: For shelf pieces, cut two 16 x 24 holes (no graph).

C: For shelf sides, cut two according to graph.

D: For beam fronts, cut four 3 x 3 holes (no graph).

E: For beam sides, cut sixteen 3 x 9 holes (no graph).

F: For pencil pot sides, cut four according to graph.

G: For cactus pot sides, cut four according to graph.

H: For pot bottoms, cut two 9 x 9 holes (no graph).

I: For cactus pot dirt, cut one 10 x 10 holes (no graph).

J: For cactus, cut one according to graph.

K: For cactus support, cut one according to graph.

L: For cactus flowers, cut seven according to graph.

M: For pepper sides, cut sixteen according to graph.

Stitching Instructions:

(**Note:** Back A and K pieces are not worked.)

1: Using colors and stitches indicated, work front A, B, F, G and M (eight on opposite side of canvas) pieces according to graphs and stitch pattern guide on page 135. Using cinnamon for beam fronts, beam sides and pot dirt, dk. rust for pot bottoms, green for cactus and Continental Stitch, work D, E and H-J pieces. With tan, Overcast cutout edges of front A; with black for shelf sides and with matching colors, Overcast edges of C, I and J pieces.

(**Note:** Separate lemon and yellow into 2-ply or nylon plastic canvas yarn into 1-ply strands.)

2: Using yellow 2-ply (or 1-ply) for three flowers and lemon 2-ply (or 1-ply) for remaining flowers, Overcast edges of L pieces. Using dk. green and Straight Stitch, embroider detail on J as indicated on graph. With thread, sew 28 bugle beads to cactus front as desired (see photo).

3: Holding back A to wrong side of front, with tan, Whipstitch together, forming Message Center Frame; Whipstitch B pieces wrong sides together, forming shelf. For each beam (make four), with cinnamon, Whipstitch one D and four E pieces together according to Beam Assembly Diagram on page 134; Overcast unfinished edges.

4: Assemble frame, shelf, C pieces and cup hooks according to Message Center Assembly Diagram on page 135. Glue beams evenly spaced to frame front across top as shown in photo.

5: For each pot, with dk. rust, Whipstitch corresponding sides and one H piece wrong sides together; Overcast edges. Glue 1-K pieces together and to inside of cactus pot as indicated and according to Cactus & Pot Assembly Diagram on page 135; glue pots to frame and shelf as shown. Glue flowers to cactus as desired (see photo).

(**Note:** Cut tan floss into four equal lengths.)

6: For each pepper, holding two M pieces wrong sides together, with forest for stem and with dk. red, Whipstitch together. For each pepper strand (make four), assemble one tan floss strand and two peppers according to Pepper Strand Assembly Diagram on page 134. Holding all four pepper strands together to hang unevenly, knot together at center. Glue knot to center of one beam (see photo).

7: Glue sawtooth hanger to back.

Frame

Cutting Instructions:

(**Notes:** Graphs on page 136. Use beige for A-C and clear canvas for remaining pieces.)

A: For front, cut one according to graph.

B: For back, cut one 34 x 45 holes (no graph).

C: For support long and short pieces, cut one 17 x 45 holes for long piece and one 15 x 17 holes for short piece (no graphs).

D: For shelf pieces, cut two 9 x 35 holes (no graph).

E: For shelf sides, cut two according to graph.

F: For beam fronts, cut three 2 x 2 holes.

G: beam sides, cut twelve 2 x 4 holes (no graph).

H: For window box sides and bottom, cut three (two for sides and one for bottom) 6 x 31 holes (no graph).

I: For window box ends, cut two 6 x 6 holes (no graph).

J: For window box dirt, cut one 5 x 30 holes (no graph).

K: For cactus leaves, cut nine according to graph.

L: For cactus supports, cut two according to graph.

Stitching Instructions:

(**Note:** B, C one H for bottom and L pieces are not worked.)

1: Using colors and stitches indicated, work A, D, F, two H pieces for sides, I and K pieces according to graphs and stitch pattern guides. Using cinnamon and Continental Stitch, work G and J pieces. With tan, Overcast cutout edges of A; with black for shelf sides and with matching colors, Overcast edges of E, J and K pieces.

2: With thread, sew six bugle beads to each cactus leaf as desired (see photo).

3: With tan, Whipstitch A-C pieces together according to Frame Assembly Diagram on page 136. Whipstitch D pieces wrong sides together, forming shelf. For each beam (make three), substituting F for D and G for E pieces, Whipstitch one F and four G pieces together according to Beam Assembly Diagram; Overcast unfinished edges.

4: Substituting E for C pieces and omitting cup hooks, glue frame, shelf and E pieces together according to Message Center Assembly Diagram; glue beams evenly spaced to Frame front across top (see photo).

5: With dk. rust Whipstitch H and I pieces together, forming window box; Overcast unfinished edges. Glue J inside window box and window box to shelf and frame (see photo). For each cactus, glue one L and five K pieces together and to one end of window box as indicated and according to Cactus Assembly Diagram on page 136.✧

A – Message Center Frame Front & Back
(cut 1 each from beige) 65 x 79 holes

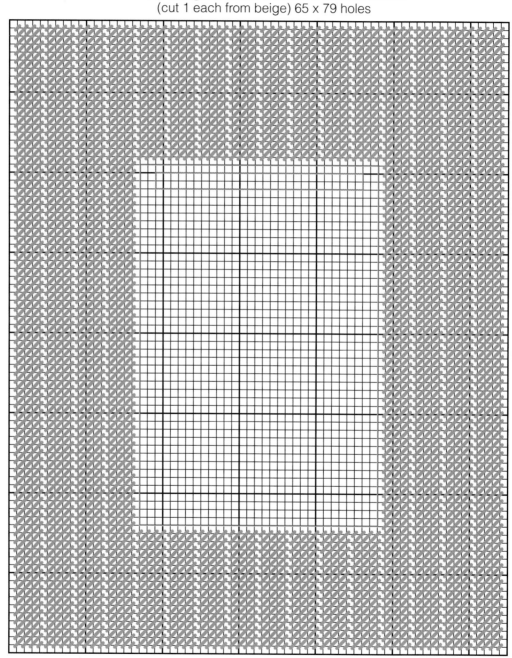

Beam Assembly Diagram

Pepper Strand Assembly Diagram

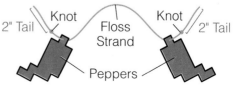

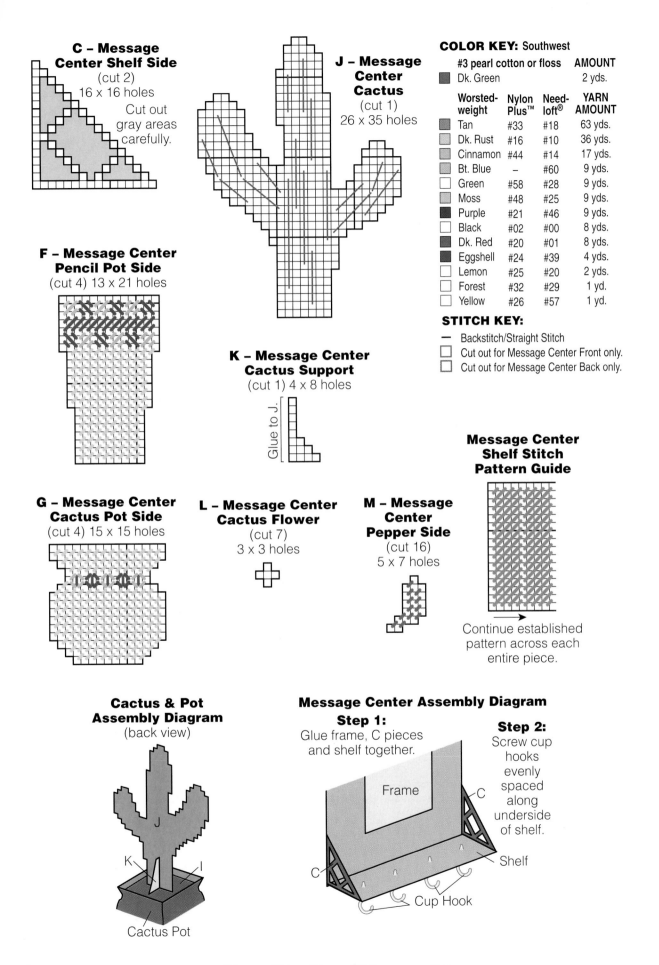

C – Message Center Shelf Side
(cut 2)
16 x 16 holes

Cut out gray areas carefully.

J – Message Center Cactus
(cut 1)
26 x 35 holes

F – Message Center Pencil Pot Side
(cut 4) 13 x 21 holes

K – Message Center Cactus Support
(cut 1) 4 x 8 holes

Glue to J.

Message Center Shelf Stitch Pattern Guide

Continue established pattern across each entire piece.

G – Message Center Cactus Pot Side
(cut 4) 15 x 15 holes

L – Message Center Cactus Flower
(cut 7)
3 x 3 holes

M – Message Center Pepper Side
(cut 16)
5 x 7 holes

Cactus & Pot Assembly Diagram
(back view)

K   J   I

Cactus Pot

Message Center Assembly Diagram

Step 1:
Glue frame, C pieces and shelf together.

Step 2:
Screw cup hooks evenly spaced along underside of shelf.

Frame

C

C

Shelf

Cup Hook

Southwestern Windows

Photo on page 129

E – Frame Shelf Side
(cut 2)
9 x 9 holes

Cut Out

F – Frame Beam Front
(cut 3)
2 x 2 holes

A – Frame Front
(cut 1) 35 x 45 holes

Cut Out

Whipstitch between arrows.

K – Frame Cactus Leaf
(cut 9) 7 x 10 holes

L – Frame Cactus Support
(cut 2) 3 x 5 holes

Glue to cactus.

Cactus Assembly Diagram
(back view)

K K K K K

L

Window Box

Frame Assembly Diagram
(back view)

Step 2:
Whipstitch opposite edge of long C to center top edge of B.

9 Holes

A

9 Holes

Step 1:
Whipstitch C pieces together at one matching edge.

Long C

B

Short C

Step 4:
Overcast unfinished edges of front.

Step 3:
Whipstitch A and B pieces wrong sides together, catching opposite edge of short C to center bottom of frame through all thicknesses as you work.

Frame Window Box Side & End Stitch Pattern Guide

Continue established pattern across each entire piece.

Frame Shelf Stitch Pattern Guide

Continue established pattern across entire piece.

COLOR KEY: Southwest

#3 pearl cotton or floss			AMOUNT
Dk. Green			2 yds.

Worsted-weight	Nylon Plus™	Need-loft®	YARN AMOUNT
Tan	#33	#18	63 yds.
Dk. Rust	#16	#10	36 yds.
Cinnamon	#44	#14	17 yds.
Bt. Blue	–	#60	9 yds.
Green	#58	#28	9 yds.
Moss	#48	#25	9 yds.
Purple	#21	#46	9 yds.
Black	#02	#00	8 yds.
Dk. Red	#20	#01	8 yds.
Eggshell	#24	#39	4 yds.
Lemon	#25	#20	2 yds.
Forest	#32	#29	1 yd.
Yellow	#26	#57	1 yd.

STITCH KEY:

– Backstitch/Straight Stitch

☐ Cut out for Message Center Front only.

☐ Cut out for Message Center Back only.

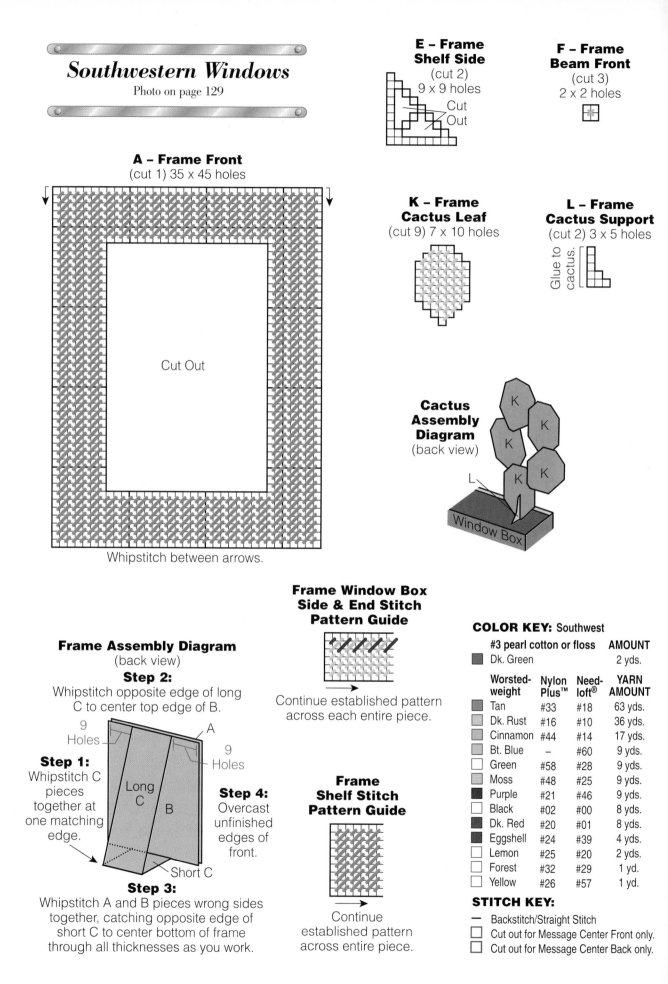

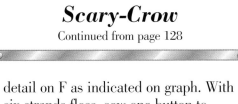

Scary-Crow

Continued from page 128

detail on F as indicated on graph. With six strands floss, sew one button to each side of A at strap areas of overalls.

3: Making long stitches as shown in photo, with six strands floss, sew J to G as indicated; sew G, H and I pieces to A as indicated.

(**Note:** Cut two 10" lengths of raffia; cut remaining raffia into 1½" - 2" pieces.)

4: Holding 10" raffia strands together, tie into a knot around hat brim on D (see photo); glue strands to wrong side to secure. Glue about 28 pieces to wrong side at bottom edge of D. Glue D to head area of A; holding right side of E to wrong side of A at matching hat points, glue E to back of A and D.

5: Glue remaining raffia pieces to bottom edge of body and inside of pocket. Glue eyes, beak, wings and feet to body as shown. Hang as desired. ✧

COLOR KEY: Scary-Crow

Embroidery floss			AMOUNT
☐ Ecru			3 yds.

Worsted-weight	Nylon Plus™	Need-loft®	YARN AMOUNT
Denim	#06	#33	45 yds.
Black	#02	#00	44 yds.
Straw	#41	#19	24 yds.
Camel	#34	#43	17 yds.
Navy	#45	#31	10 yds.
Dusty Blue	#38	#34	8 yds.
Cinnamon	#44	#14	6 yds.
Red	#19	#02	2 yds.
☐ White	#01	#41	1 yd.

STITCH KEY:

— Backstitch/Straight Stitch
☐ Patch Placement
☐ Pocket Placement

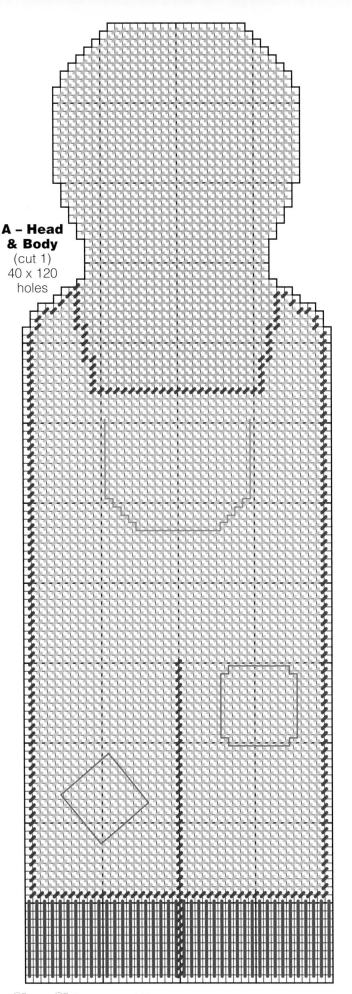

A – Head & Body
(cut 1)
40 x 120 holes

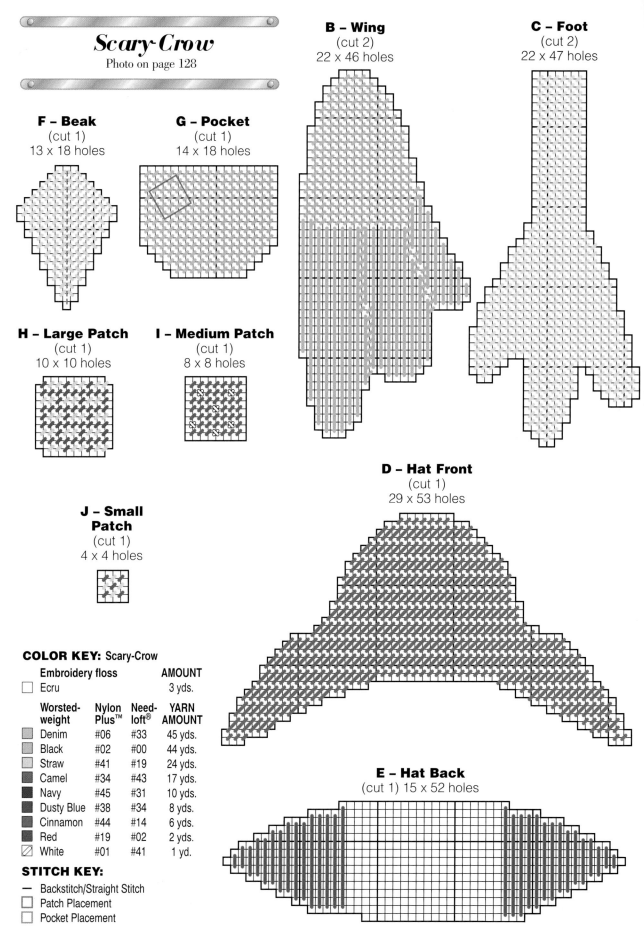

Scary-Crow
Photo on page 128

B – Wing
(cut 2)
22 x 46 holes

C – Foot
(cut 2)
22 x 47 holes

F – Beak
(cut 1)
13 x 18 holes

G – Pocket
(cut 1)
14 x 18 holes

H – Large Patch
(cut 1)
10 x 10 holes

I – Medium Patch
(cut 1)
8 x 8 holes

J – Small Patch
(cut 1)
4 x 4 holes

D – Hat Front
(cut 1)
29 x 53 holes

COLOR KEY: Scary-Crow

Embroidery floss			AMOUNT
☐ Ecru			3 yds.

	Worsted-weight	Nylon Plus™	Need-loft®	YARN AMOUNT
☐	Denim	#06	#33	45 yds.
■	Black	#02	#00	44 yds.
☐	Straw	#41	#19	24 yds.
■	Camel	#34	#43	17 yds.
■	Navy	#45	#31	10 yds.
■	Dusty Blue	#38	#34	8 yds.
■	Cinnamon	#44	#14	6 yds.
■	Red	#19	#02	2 yds.
☐	White	#01	#41	1 yd.

STITCH KEY:
— Backstitch/Straight Stitch
☐ Patch Placement
☐ Pocket Placement

E – Hat Back
(cut 1) 15 x 52 holes

ULTIMATE

Christmas Cheer

COLLECTION

Poinsettia Card Caddy

Designed by Joyce Messenger

Size:
3⅞" x 7½" x 5¾" tall.

Materials:
1½ sheets of clear and ½ sheet of green 7-count plastic canvas; One artificial holly berry sprig and one holly leaf; Three yellow 11-mm tri-beads; Craft glue or glue gun; Worsted-weight or plastic canvas yarn (for amounts see Color Key).

Cutting Instructions:
(**Note:** Use green for E and clear canvas for remaining pieces.)

A: For back, cut one 37 x 49 holes.
B: For front, cut one according to graph.
C: For side #1, cut one according to graph.
D: For side #2, cut one 23 x 25 holes (no graph).
E: For bottom, cut one from green 25 x 49 holes (no graph).
F: For leaves, cut four according to graph.
G: For poinsettia bracts, cut six according to graph.

Stitching Instructions:
(**Note:** E piece is not worked.)

1: Using colors and stitches indicated, work A-C, F and G pieces according to graphs; work D according to pattern established on B. With matching colors, Overcast edges of F and G pieces.

2: Using red and Straight Stitch, embroider detail on A as indicated on graph.

3: With fern, Whipstitch A-E pieces together as indicated and according to Card Caddy

Assembly Diagram; Overcast unfinished edges.

4: For each flower (make three), glue two G pieces together; glue one bead to center as shown in photo. Glue flowers and F pieces to front and artificial leaf and berry sprig to back as shown.✧

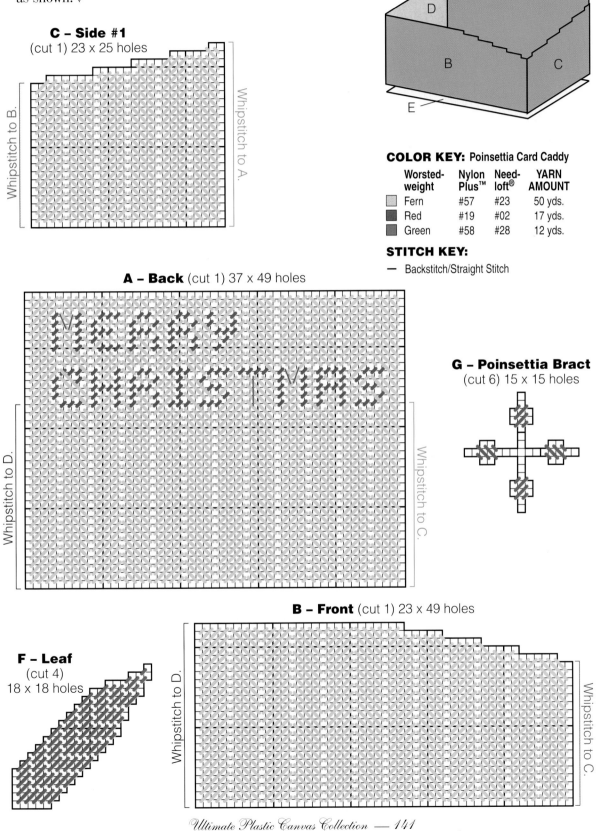

Card Caddy Assembly Diagram

C – Side #1
(cut 1) 23 x 25 holes

Whipstitch to B.

Whipstitch to A.

COLOR KEY: Poinsettia Card Caddy

	Worsted-weight	Nylon Plus™	Need-loft®	YARN AMOUNT
	Fern	#57	#23	50 yds.
	Red	#19	#02	17 yds.
	Green	#58	#28	12 yds.

STITCH KEY:
— Backstitch/Straight Stitch

A – Back (cut 1) 37 x 49 holes

Whipstitch to D.

Whipstitch to C.

G – Poinsettia Bract
(cut 6) 15 x 15 holes

F – Leaf
(cut 4)
18 x 18 holes

B – Front (cut 1) 23 x 49 holes

Whipstitch to D.

Whipstitch to C.

Celestial Christmas Orb

Designed by Carol Nartowicz

Size:
About 11" across with lights in place.

Materials:
Twelve 5" plastic canvas star shapes by Uniek® Crafts; String of miniature lights with at least 30 bulbs; Monofilament fishing line (for optional hanger); Craft glue or glue gun; Metallic cord (for amount see Color Key); Raffia straw (for amounts see Color Key).

Cutting Instructions:
A: For sides, cut 12 star shapes according to graph.

Stitching Instructions:
1: Using colors and stitches indicated (work silver Continental Stitches first), work four pieces in each of the following color combinations according to graph: two green, two white, one red point; two green, two red, one white point; two red, two white, one green point. Do not Overcast cutout edges.

2: Omitting tip edges, with metallic cord, Whipstitch 11 pieces together, forming a ball. Placing lights inside globe, push one light through each center cutout and point opening; glue sockets, not bulbs, to secure.

3: Omitting edges on last tip, Whipstitch remaining side in place. Position and glue lights through four finished points and center; push any remaining bulbs into center of ball. With cord extending through last point (tack in place on inside to secure), Whipstitch remaining straight edges together.

4: For optional hanger, thread a double strand of fishing line through one edge at one point; tie ends together and glue knot to secure. ✧

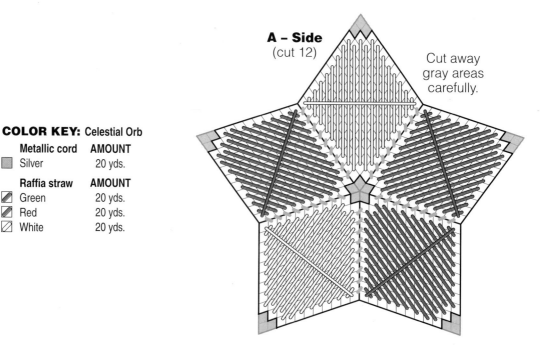

A – Side
(cut 12)

Cut away gray areas carefully.

COLOR KEY: Celestial Orb

Metallic cord	AMOUNT
Silver	20 yds.

Raffia straw	AMOUNT
Green	20 yds.
Red	20 yds.
White	20 yds.

*Reach for the stars and
light up the season with
a geometric star
from the East.*

Hear the merry chatter of Santa and his elves at work making gifts in his north pole cottage toy shop.

Santa's Toy Shop

Designed by Nancy Dorman

Size:
Snugly covers a boutique-style tissue box.

Materials:
Three sheets of 7-count plastic canvas; ½ sheet of 10-count plastic canvas; Two round wooden toothpicks; One miniature teddy bear; ½ yd. green ¹⁄₁₆" satin ribbon; ¾ yd. red ⅛" satin ribbon; ¼ yd. gold ⅛" ribbon; 6" length of 16-gauge wire; Polyester fiberfill; Craft glue or glue gun; Six-strand embroidery floss (for amounts see Color Key on page 147); Heavy metallic braid or metallic cord (for amount see Color Key); Worsted-weight or plastic canvas yarn (for amounts see Color Key).

Cutting Instructions:
(**Notes:** Graphs & Diagrams on pages 146-148. Cut L-W pieces from 10-count and remaining pieces from 7-count canvas.)

A: For base, cut one according to graph.
B: For shop front, cut one according to graph.
C: For shop back, cut one according to graph.
D: For shop sides, cut two 31 x 35 holes.
E: For roof sides, cut two according to graph.

F: For chimney front and back, cut two (one for front and one for back) according to graph.

G: For chimney sides, cut two 11 x 13 holes.

H: For roof front and back trims, cut two (one for front and one for back) according to graph.

I: For roof side trims, cut two according to graph.

J: For porch roof pieces, cut two 7 x 14 holes (no graph).

K: For shutters, cut six 4 x 12 holes (no graph).

L: For sign, cut one according to graph.

M: For candy canes, cut two according to graph.

N: For door wreath, cut one according to graph.

O: For window wreaths, cut three according to graph.

P: For stocking, cut one according to graph.

Q: For gift, cut one 4 x 7 holes (no graph).

R: For drum side, cut one 3 x 16 holes.

S: For drum top and bottom, cut two (one for top and one for bottom) according to graph.

T: For mailbox top, cut one 10 x 12 holes.

U: For mailbox bottom, cut one 4 x 10 holes (no graph).

V: For mailbox ends, cut two according to graph.

W: For mailbox flag, cut one according to graph.

Stitching Instructions:

(**Note:** W piece is not worked.)

1: Using colors and stitches indicated, work A-J pieces according to graphs and stitch pattern guide; fill in uncoded areas of B-D pieces using green and Continental Stitch. Using red and Slanted Gobelin Stitch over narrow width, work K pieces. With matching colors, Overcast edges of A and K pieces.

2: Using yarn, braid or cord and six strands floss in colors and embroidery stitches indicated, embroider window panes on C and D pieces and door panels and doorknob on B as indicated on graphs.

(**Note:** Use Herringbone Whipstitch for Whipstitch.)

3: With green, Whipstitch B-D pieces together according to Shop Assembly Diagram on page 147; with white for bottom edges and with green, Overcast unfinished edges.

4: With white, Whipstitch E, H and I pieces together according to Roof Assembly Diagram; Overcast unfinished edges.

5: With red, Whipstitch F and G pieces together according to Chimney Assembly Diagram; with white for top and with red, Overcast unfinished edges.

6: With white, Whipstitch J pieces together at one short end, forming porch roof; Overcast unfinished edges.

7: With red, tack shutters to house sides and back as indicated and chimney to roof. With white, tack porch roof to shop front as indicated, roof to shop top and shop to cutout opening of base.

(**Notes:** Separate remaining yarn into 2-ply or nylon plastic canvas yarn into 1-ply strands. Do not use Herringbone Whipstitch for Whipstitch.)

8: Using 2-ply (or 1-ply) yarn in colors and stitches indicated, work M-P, S and V pieces according to graphs. Using white for sign, braid or cord for gift, green for drum side, red for mailbox top and mailbox bottom and Continental Stitch, work L, Q, R, T and U pieces.

9: With red for sign and candles on window wreaths, braid or cord for candle flames on window wreaths, white for candy canes, green for mailbox flag and with matching colors, Overcast edges of L-Q and W pieces. Using yarn, braid or cord and six strands floss in colors and embroidery stitches indicated, embroider letters on L and T pieces, holly berries on N and O pieces and detail on P and R pieces as indicated.

10: With green, Whipstitch ends of R together as indicated; with red, Whipstitch R and S pieces together, forming drum. For drumsticks, cut one toothpick in half; glue halves to top of drum as shown in photo.

11: For mailbox, with red, Whipstitch T-V pieces together as indicated and according to Mailbox Assembly Diagram on page 148; Overcast unfinished edges. For mailbox stand, wrap one toothpick with red yarn until completely covered; glue ends to secure. Glue stand and mailbox flag to mailbox as shown.

CONTINUED ON PAGE 146

(**Note:** Cut wire into two equal lengths.)

12: For each candy cane, holding one wire to wrong side of one M, glue in place; tack one candy cane to each corner of porch roof and to base as shown.

(**Notes:** Cut green ribbon into two equal lengths; cut red ribbon into three equal lengths. Tie individual ribbons and remaining braid or cord into bow; trim ends.)

13: Glue one green ribbon to gift and one to teddy bear; glue one red ribbon to each window wreath as shown. Glue gold bow to door wreath and braid bow to gift as shown.

14: For snow, glue fiberfill to base around shop as shown. For note, write "Santa" on a small piece of paper and glue inside mailbox. Glue sign and wreaths to house and stocking, drum, gift, teddy bear and mailbox assembly to base as shown. ✧

B – Shop Front
(cut 1)
31 x 50 holes

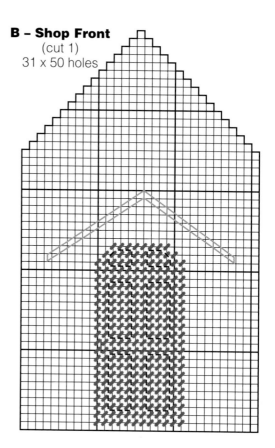

C – Shop Back
(cut 1)
31 x 50 holes

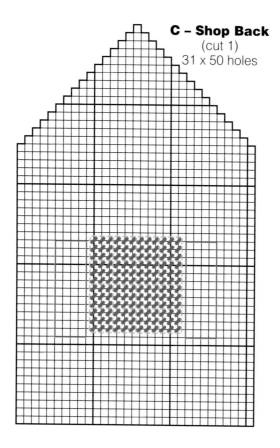

D – Shop Side (cut 2) 31 x 35 holes

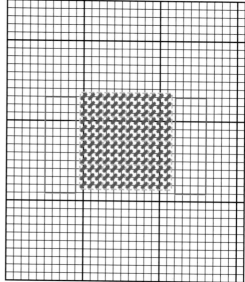

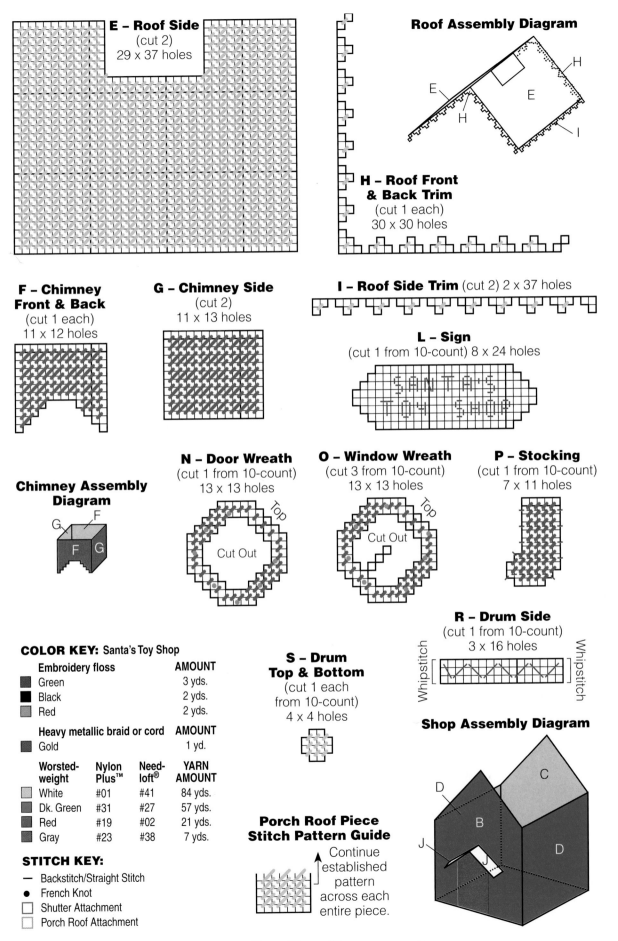

E – Roof Side
(cut 2)
29 x 37 holes

Roof Assembly Diagram

H – Roof Front & Back Trim
(cut 1 each)
30 x 30 holes

F – Chimney Front & Back
(cut 1 each)
11 x 12 holes

G – Chimney Side
(cut 2)
11 x 13 holes

I – Roof Side Trim (cut 2) 2 x 37 holes

L – Sign
(cut 1 from 10-count) 8 x 24 holes

Chimney Assembly Diagram

N – Door Wreath
(cut 1 from 10-count)
13 x 13 holes

Cut Out

O – Window Wreath
(cut 3 from 10-count)
13 x 13 holes

Cut Out

P – Stocking
(cut 1 from 10-count)
7 x 11 holes

R – Drum Side
(cut 1 from 10-count)
3 x 16 holes

Whipstitch

Whipstitch

COLOR KEY: Santa's Toy Shop

Embroidery floss			AMOUNT
Green			3 yds.
Black			2 yds.
Red			2 yds.

Heavy metallic braid or cord			AMOUNT
Gold			1 yd.

Worsted-weight	Nylon Plus™	Need-loft®	YARN AMOUNT
White	#01	#41	84 yds.
Dk. Green	#31	#27	57 yds.
Red	#19	#02	21 yds.
Gray	#23	#38	7 yds.

STITCH KEY:
— Backstitch/Straight Stitch
● French Knot
☐ Shutter Attachment
☐ Porch Roof Attachment

S – Drum Top & Bottom
(cut 1 each from 10-count)
4 x 4 holes

Porch Roof Piece Stitch Pattern Guide

Continue established pattern across each entire piece.

Shop Assembly Diagram

Santa's Toy Shop

Photo on page 144

T – Mailbox Top
(cut 1 from 10-count)
10 x 12 holes

Whipstitch to U.

Whipstitch to U.

Whipstitch to one V.

V – Mailbox End
(cut 2 from 10-count)
4 x 4 holes

Whipstitch to U.

W – Mailbox Flag
(cut 1 from 10-count)
3 x 6 holes

Mailbox Assembly Diagram

V

T

V

U

COLOR KEY: Santa's Toy Shop

Embroidery floss			AMOUNT
Green			3 yds.
Black			2 yds.
Red			2 yds.

Heavy metallic braid or cord			AMOUNT
Gold			1 yd.

Worsted-weight	Nylon Plus™	Need-loft®	YARN AMOUNT
White	#01	#41	84 yds.
Dk. Green	#31	#27	57 yds.
Red	#19	#02	21 yds.
Gray	#23	#38	7 yds.

STITCH KEY:
- — Backstitch/Straight Stitch
- ● French Knot
- □ Shutter Attachment
- □ Porch Roof Attachment

M – Candy Cane
(cut 2 from 10-count)
9 x 30 holes

A – Base (cut 1) 61 x 61 holes

Cut Out

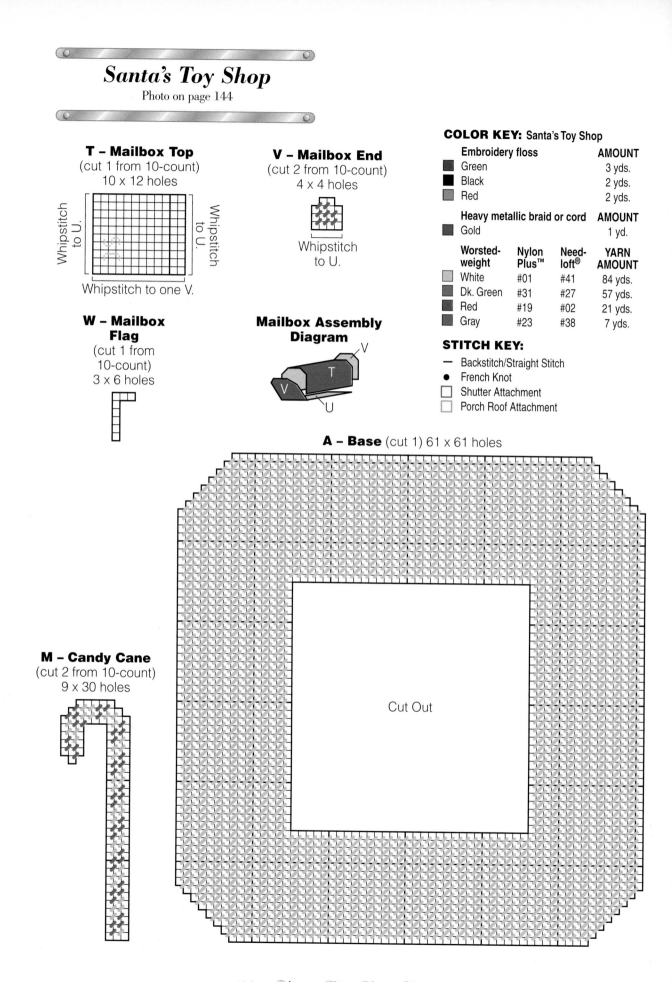

Musical Lights

Designed by Cherie Marie Leck

Size:
Angel is 4" x 4¾"; Tree is 3½" x 5½".

Materials:
½ sheet of 5-count plastic canvas; One yellow single-light music button with holiday tune of choice: one multi-colored 6-light music button with holiday tune of choice; Craft glue or glue gun; Metallic cord (for amounts see Color Key on page 154); Worsted-weight or plastic canvas yarn (for amounts see Color Key).

Cutting Instructions:
(**Note:** Graphs on page 154.)

A: For Angel front and backing, cut two (one for front and one for backing) according to graph.

B: For Tree front and backing, cut two (one for front and one for backing) according to graph.

Stitching Instructions:
(**Notes:** Backing pieces are not worked. Use a double strand of yarn and cord except for embroidery.)

1: Using colors and stitches indicated, work one A and one B for fronts according to graphs.

2: Using dk. brown and Straight Stitch, embroider eyes on front A as indicated on graph. Using cord and loose Straight Stitches, embroider garland on front B as indicated; glue cord to tree to secure.

3: For Angel, holding gold area of single light music button to wrong side of front A, push yellow light from back to front through ◆ hole as indicated; coil excess wire to lay flat between light and button. Holding backing A to wrong side of front with music button assembly between, with matching colors, Whipstitch together.

4: For Tree, holding gold area of 6-light music button to wrong side of front B, push lights from back to front through ▲ holes as indicated. Holding backing B to wrong side of front with music button assembly between, with forest for tree branches, yellow for star (see photo) and with dk. red, Whipstitch together.✧

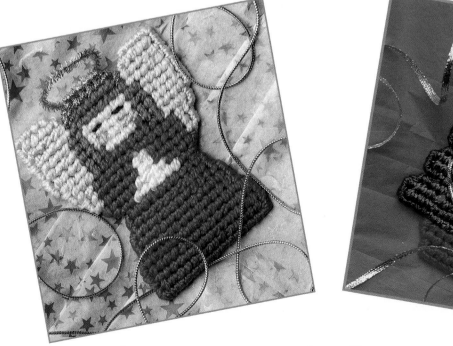

Starbright Angel

Designed by Sandra Miller Maxfield

Size:
About 6¼" x 9".

Materials:
One sheet of 7-count plastic canvas; White craft feathers, ⅓ yd. off-white 1" lace trim; 1½ yds. gold glitter sequin string; ½ yd. gold metallic cord; One 1" jingle bell; One wooden 1" bead; Blonde curly doll hair; Craft glue or glue gun; Worsted-weight or plastic canvas yarn (for amounts see Color Key).

Cutting Instructions:
A: For head front and back, cut two (one for front and one for back) according to graph.

B: For dress pieces, cut two according to graph.

C: For sleeve pieces, cut four according to graph.

D: For leg fronts and backs, cut two each according to graphs.

E: For hand pieces, cut four 3 x 4 holes.

F: For wings, cut one according to graph.

Stitching Instructions:
1: Using colors and stitches indicated, work one A for front and B-F pieces according to graphs; using lt. pink and Continental Stitch, work remaining A for back. With white, Overcast edges of F.

2: For head, holding A pieces wrong sides together, with lt. pink, Whipstitch together as indicated on graph; Overcast unfinished edges. For dress, holding B pieces wrong sides together, with royal, Whipstitch together as indicated; for each sleeve, holding two C pieces wrong sides together, Whipstitch together as indicated. Overcast unfinished edges of dress and sleeves.

3: For each leg, holding one of each D wrong sides together, with matching colors, Whipstitch together. For each hand, holding two E pieces wrong sides together, with lt. pink, Whipstitch together.

4: Slip open edges of head over neck area of dress; glue to secure. Glue sleeves to back of dress at bodice area and one hand inside each cuff opening of sleeves as shown in photo.

5: Glue lace around bottom edge of dress and at neckline for collar; glue sequin string around hemline lace, cuffs and neckline as shown in photo. Glue hair to head and sequin string around top of head for halo as shown.

6: Omitting center area, glue feathers to wings; glue sequins to top of wing feathers as shown

and wings to back of dress at bodice area.
(**Note:** Cut metallic cord in half.)

7: For loop hanger, tie ends of one cord strand together; glue knot to center back at top of head.

8: To attach legs, assemble legs, bell and bead according to Legs Assembly Diagram; glue wooden bead to inside of dress just below waist area, and glue legs to inside back of dress to secure. ✧

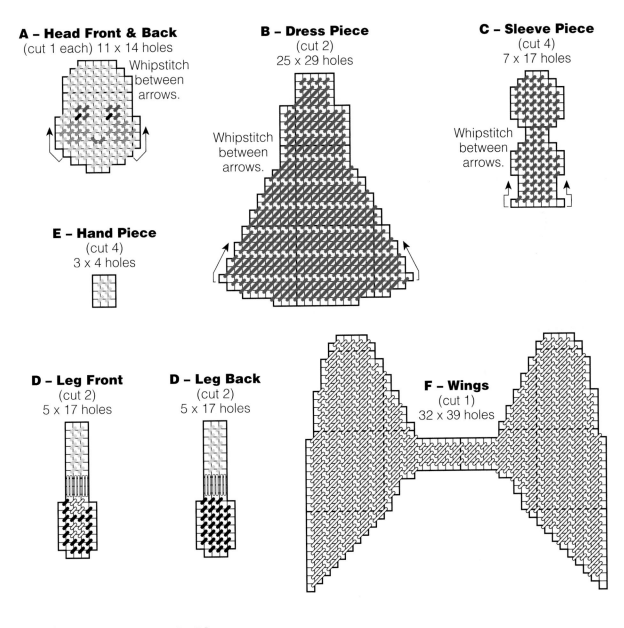

A – Head Front & Back
(cut 1 each) 11 x 14 holes

Whipstitch between arrows.

E – Hand Piece
(cut 4)
3 x 4 holes

B – Dress Piece
(cut 2)
25 x 29 holes

Whipstitch between arrows.

C – Sleeve Piece
(cut 4)
7 x 17 holes

Whipstitch between arrows.

D – Leg Front
(cut 2)
5 x 17 holes

D – Leg Back
(cut 2)
5 x 17 holes

F – Wings
(cut 1)
32 x 39 holes

Legs Assembly Diagram

Step 1:
Thread cord from back to front through center top of one leg; knot end on back to secure.

Bead
Bell
Cord
3/4"
Leg

Step 2:
Leaving about 3/4" of cord between bell and each leg, thread cord through bell loop, then through bead, through bell loop again; thread cord from front to back through remaining leg and knot end on back.

COLOR KEY: Starbright Angel

	Worsted-weight	Nylon Plus™	Need-loft®	YARN AMOUNT
■	Royal	#09	#32	23 yds.
▨	White	#01	#41	20 yds.
▨	Lt. Pink	#10	#08	9 yds.
■	Black	#02	#00	3 yds.
▨	Pink	#11	#07	1/2 yd.
■	Red	#19	#02	1/4 yd.

Holiday Faces Ornaments

Designed by Johnna Miller

Size:
Each has a 1" x 1¼" photo window.

Materials:
½ sheet of green, ¼ sheet each of yellow, blue and red, and scraps of clear and white 7-count plastic canvas; ½" gold jingle bell; ¼ yd. each dk. green and red ⅛" satin ribbon; Nine red 5-mm and three red 20-mm pom-poms; One yellow star pony bead; ⅔ yd. gold twisted metallic thread or fine metallic braid; Craft glue or glue gun; Worsted-weight or plastic canvas yarn (for amounts see Color Key).

Cutting Instructions:
(**Note:** Graphs continued on page 154.)

A: For Bell front and back, cut one each from yellow according to graphs.

B: For Wreath front and back, cut one each from green according to graphs.

C: For Holly Leaf front and back, cut one each from green according to graphs.

D: For Tree front and back, cut one each from green according to graphs.

E: For Mitten front and back, cut one each from blue according to graphs.

F: For Mitten cuff, cut one from white 2 x 9 holes.

G: For Sled front and back, cut one each from red according to graphs.

H: For Sled runner pieces, cut four from clear according to graph.

Stitching Instructions:

1: Using colors indicated and Continental Stitch, work pieces (two H pieces on opposite side of canvas) according to graphs; with matching colors, Overcast edges of A-G pieces.

2: For each runner, holding two H pieces wrong sides together, with silver, Whipstitch together.

(Note: Cut six 3" lengths of thread or braid.

3: For each hanger, thread one 3" strand of thread or braid through center top of each front piece; knot ends together.

(Notes: Cut one 1½" length of thread or braid. Tie ribbons into bows and trim ends.)

4: For Bell, thread jingle bell on 1½" strand of thread or braid; glue ends to wrong side of back A at center bottom. Glue A pieces wrong sides together (center back over front) with photo between centered over front cutout; glue green bow to top of Bell Ornament as shown in photo.

5: For each Ornament, glue corresponding front and back pieces wrong sides together (center back over front) with photo between centered over front cutout.

6: Glue red bow and small pom-poms to Wreath; glue large pom-poms to Holly Leaf, star bead to Tree and F to Mitten as shown. Glue runners to bottom of Sled as indicated. ✥

COLOR KEY: Holiday Faces

	Worsted-weight	Nylon Plus™	Need-loft®	YARN AMOUNT
■	Dk. Green	#31	#27	18 yds.
■	Royal	#09	#32	8 yds.
■	Yellow	#26	#57	8 yds.
■	Dk. Red	#20	#01	6 yds.
■	Silver	#40	#37	4 yds.
▨	White	#01	#41	1 yd.
■	Cinnamon	#44	#14	½ yd.

STITCH KEY:
— Runner Placement

A – Bell Front
(cut 1 from yellow)
17 x 19 holes

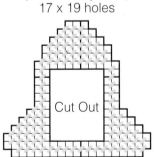

B – Wreath Front
(cut 1 from green)
17 x 17 holes

B – Wreath Back
(cut 1 from green)
16 x 16 holes

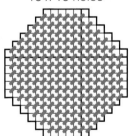

A – Bell Back
(cut 1 from yellow)
16 x 18 holes

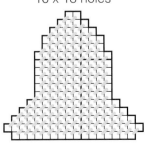

C – Holly Leaf Front
(cut 1 from green)
15 x 22 holes

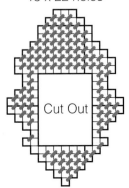

C – Holly Leaf Back
(cut 1 from green)
14 x 20 holes

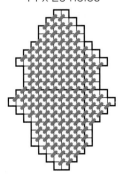

Holiday Faces Ornaments

Photo on page 152

G – Sled Front
(cut 1 from red)
11 x 18 holes

Cut Out

G – Sled Back
(cut 1 from red)
8 x 16 holes

D – Tree Front
(cut 1 from green)
19 x 20 holes

Cut Out

D – Tree Back
(cut 1 from green)
17 x 18 holes

F – Mitten Cuff
(cut 1 from white)
2 x 9 holes

H – Sled Runner Piece
(cut 4 from clear)
4 x 21 holes

Glue to Sled.

E – Mitten Front
(cut 1 from blue)
18 x 19 holes

Cut Out

E – Mitten Back
(cut 1 from blue)
17 x 18 holes

COLOR KEY: Holiday Faces

	Worsted-weight	Nylon Plus™	Need-loft®	YARN AMOUNT
	Dk. Green	#31	#27	18 yds.
	Royal	#09	#32	8 yds.
	Yellow	#26	#57	8 yds.
	Dk. Red	#20	#01	6 yds.
	Silver	#40	#37	4 yds.
⊘	White	#01	#41	1 yd.
	Cinnamon	#44	#14	1/2 yd.

STITCH KEY:
— Runner Placement

Musical Lights

Photo on page 149

A – Angel Front & Backing
(cut 1 each) 19 x 23 holes

B – Tree Front & Backing
(cut 1 each)
17 x 27 holes

COLOR KEY: Musical Lights

	Metallic cord			AMOUNT
	Gold			1 yd.
	Silver			1/2 yd.

	Worsted-weight	Nylon Plus™	Need-loft®	YARN AMOUNT
	Dk. Green	#31	#27	8 yds.
	Bt. Purple	–	#64	7 yds.
	Silver	#40	#37	5 yds.
	Forest	#32	#29	3 yds.
	Dk. Red	#20	#01	2 yds.
	Maple	#35	#13	2 yds.
	Royal	#09	#32	2 yds.
	Flesh	#14	#56	1 yd.
	Dk. Brown	#36	#15	1/2 yd.
	Pink	#11	#07	1/2 yd.
	White	#01	#41	1/2 yd.
	Yellow	#26	#57	1/2 yd.

STITCH KEY:
— Backstitch/Straight Stitch

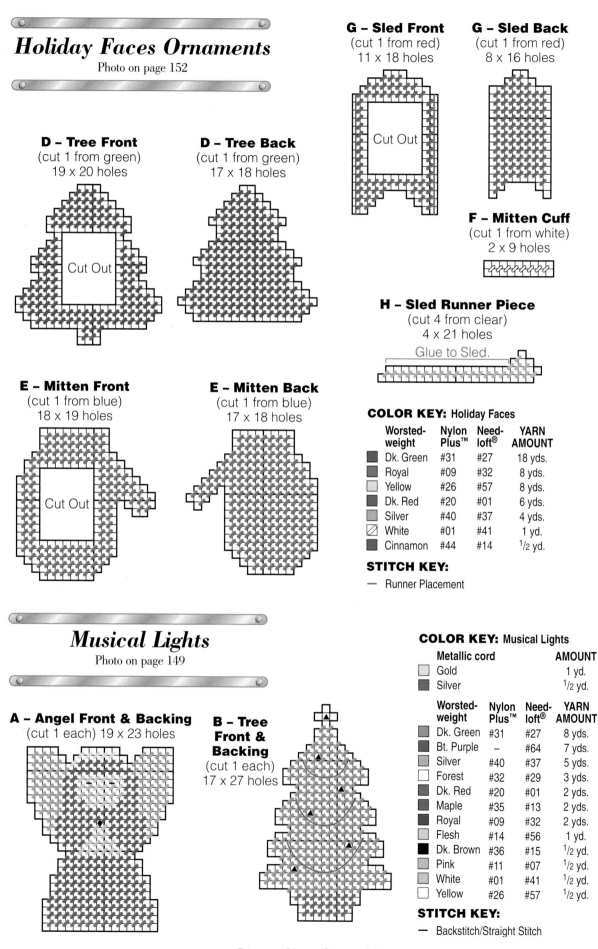

Ready, Set, Stitch

Basic Instructions to Get You Started

Most plastic canvas stitchers love getting their projects organized before they even step out the door in search of supplies. A few moments of careful planning can make the creation of your project even more fun.

First of all, prepare your work area. You will need a flat surface for cutting and assembly, and you will need a place to store your materials. Good lighting is essential, and a comfortable chair will make your stitching time even more enjoyable.

Do you plan to make one project, or will you be making several of the same item? A materials list appears at the beginning of each pattern. If you plan to make several of the same item, multiply your materials accordingly. Your shopping list is ready.

Canvas

Most projects can be made using standard-size sheets of canvas. Standard-size sheets of 7-count (7 holes per inch) are always 70 x 90 holes and are about 10½" x 13½". For larger projects, 7-count canvas also comes in 12" x 18" (80 x 120 holes) and 13½" x 22½" (90 x 150 holes) sheets. Other shapes are available in 7-count, including circles, diamonds, purse forms and ovals.

10-count canvas (10 holes per inch) comes only in standard-size sheets, which vary slightly depending on brand. They are 10½" x 13½" (106 x 136 holes) or 11" x 14" (108 x 138 holes).

5-count canvas (5 holes per inch) and 14-count (14 holes per inch) sheets are also available.

Some canvas is soft and pliable, while other canvas is stiffer and more rigid. To prevent canvas from cracking during or after stitching, you'll want to choose pliable canvas for projects that require shaping, like round baskets with curved handles. For easier shaping, warm canvas pieces with a blow-dry hair dryer to soften; dip in cool water to set. If your project is a box or an item that will stand alone, stiffer canvas is more suitable.

Both 7- and 10-count canvas sheets are available in a rainbow of colors. Most designs can be stitched on colored as well as clear canvas. When a pattern does not specify color in the materials list, you can assume clear canvas was used in the photographed model. If you'd like to stitch only a portion of the design, leaving a portion unstitched, use colored canvas to coordinate with yarn colors.

Buy the same brand of canvas for each entire project. Different brands of canvas may differ slightly in the distance between each bar.

Marking & Counting Tools

To avoid wasting canvas, careful cutting of each piece is important. For some pieces with square corners, you might be comfortable cutting the canvas without marking it beforehand. But for pieces with lots of angles and cutouts, you may want to mark your canvas before cutting.

Always count before you mark and cut. To count holes on the graphs, look for the bolder lines showing each ten holes. These ten-count lines begin in the lower left-hand corner of each graph and are on the graph to make counting easier. To count holes on the canvas, you may use your tapestry needle, a toothpick or a plastic hair roller pick. Insert the needle or pick slightly in each hole as you count.

Most stitchers have tried a variety of marking tools and have settled on a favorite, which may be crayon, permanent marker, grease pencil or ball point pen. One of the best marking tools is a fine-point overhead projection marker, available at office supply stores. The ink is dark and easy to see and washes off completely with water. After cutting and before stitching, it's important to remove all marks so they won't stain yarn as you stitch or show through stitches later. Cloth and paper toweling removes grease pencil and crayon marks, as do fabric softener sheets that have already been used in your dryer.

Supplies

Yarn, canvas, needles, cutters and most other supplies needed to complete the projects in this book are available at craft and needlework stores and through mail order catalogs. Other supplies are available at fabric, hardware and discount stores. For mail order information, see page 157.

CUTTING TOOLS

You may find it very helpful to have several tools on hand for cutting canvas. When cutting long, straight sections, scissors, craft cutters or kitchen shears are the fastest and easiest to use. For cutting out detailed areas and trimming nubs, you may like using manicure scissors or nail clippers. Many stitchers love using Ultimate Plastic Canvas Cutters, available only from *The Needlecraft Shop* catalog. If you prefer laying your canvas flat when cutting, try a craft knife and cutting surface – self-healing mats designed for sewing and kitchen cutting boards work well.

YARN AND OTHER STITCHING MATERIALS

You may choose two-ply nylon plastic canvas yarn (the color numbers of two popular brands are found in the general materials lists and Color Keys) or four-ply worsted-weight yarn for stitching on 7-count canvas. There are about 42 yards per ounce of plastic canvas yarn and 50 yards per ounce of worsted-weight yarn.

Worsted-weight yarn is widely available and comes in wool, acrylic, cotton and blends. If you decide to use worsted-weight yarn, choose 100% acrylic for best coverage. Select worsted-weight yarn by color instead of the color names or numbers found in the Color Keys. Projects stitched with worsted-weight yarn often "fuzz" after use. "Fuzz" can be removed by shaving it off with a fabric shaver to make your project look new again.

Plastic canvas yarn comes in about 60 colors and is a favorite of many plastic canvas designers. These yarns "wear" well both while stitching and in the finished product. When buying plastic canvas yarn, shop using the color names or numbers found in the Color Keys, or select colors of your choice.

To cover 5-count canvas, use a doubled strand of worsted-weight or plastic canvas yarn.

Choose sport-weight yarn or #3 pearl cotton for stitching on 10-count canvas. To cover 10-count canvas using six-strand embroidery floss, use 12 strands held together. Single and double plies of yarn will also cover 10-count and can be used for embroidery or accent stitching worked over needlepoint stitches – simply separate worsted-weight yarn into 2-ply or plastic canvas yarn into 1-ply. Nylon plastic canvas yarn does not perform as well as knitting worsted when separated and can be frustrating to use, but it is possible. Just use short lengths, separate into single plies and twist each ply slightly.

Embroidery floss or #5 pearl cotton can also be used for embroidery, and each covers 14-count canvas well.

Metallic cord is a tightly-woven cord that comes in dozens of glittering colors. Some are solid-color metallics, including gold and silver, and some have colors interwoven with gold or silver threads. If your metallic cord has a white core, the core may be removed for super-easy stitching. To do so, cut a length of cord; grasp center core fibers with tweezers or fingertips and pull. Core slips out easily. Though the sparkly look of metallics will add much to your project, you may substitute contrasting colors of yarn.

Natural and synthetic raffia straw will cover 7-count canvas if flattened before stitching. Use short lengths to prevent splitting, and glue ends to prevent unraveling.

CUTTING CANVAS

Follow all Cutting Instructions, Notes and labels above graphs to cut canvas. Each piece is labeled with a letter of the alphabet. Square-sided pieces are cut according to hole count, and some may not have a graph.

Unlike sewing patterns, graphs are not designed to be used as actual patterns but rather as counting, cutting and stitching guides. Therefore, graphs may not be actual size. Count the holes on the graph (see Marking & Counting Tools on page 155), mark your canvas to match, then cut. The old carpenters' adage – "Measure twice, cut once" – is good advice. Trim off the nubs close to the bar, and trim all corners diagonally.

For large projects, as you cut each piece, it is a good idea to label it with its letter and name. Use sticky labels, or fasten scrap paper notes through the canvas with a twist tie or a quick stitch with a scrap of yarn. To stay organized, you many want to store corresponding pieces together in zip-close bags.

If you want to make several of a favorite design to give as gifts or sell at bazaars, make cutting canvas easier and faster by making a master pattern. From colored canvas, cut out one of each piece required. For duplicates, place the colored canvas on top of clear canvas and cut out. If needed, secure the canvas pieces together with paper fasteners, twist ties or yarn. By using this method, you only have to count from the graphs once.

If you accidentally cut or tear a bar or two on your canvas, don't worry! Boo-boos can usually be repaired in one of several ways: heat the tip of a metal skewer and melt the canvas back together; glue torn bars with a tiny drop of craft glue, super glue or hot glue; or reinforce the torn section with a separate piece of canvas placed at the back of your work. When reinforcing with extra canvas, stitch through both thicknesses.

NEEDLES & OTHER STITCHING TOOLS

Blunt-end tapestry needles are used for stitching plastic canvas. Choose a No. 16 needle for stitching 5- and 7-count, a No. 18 for stitching 10-count and a No. 24 for stitching 14-count canvas. A small pair of embroidery scissors for snipping yarn is handy. Try using needle-nosed jewelry pliers for pulling the needle through several thicknesses of canvas and out of tight spots too small for your hand.

STITCHING THE CANVAS

Stitching Instructions for each section are found after the Cutting Instructions. First, refer to the illustrations of basic stitches found on page 158 to familiarize yourself with the stitches used. Illustrations will be found near the graphs for pieces worked using special stitches. Follow the numbers on the tiny graph beside the illustration to make each stitch – bring your needle up from the back of the work on odd numbers and down through the front of the work on the even numbers.

Before beginning, read the Stitching Instructions to get an overview of what you'll be doing. You'll find that some pieces are stitched using colors and stitches indicated on graphs, and for other pieces you will be given a color and stitch to use to cover the entire piece.

Cut yarn lengths between 18" to 36". Thread needle; do not tie a knot in the end. Bring your needle up through the canvas from the back, leaving a short length of yarn on the wrong side of the canvas. As you begin to stitch, work over this short length of yarn. If you are beginning with Continental Stitches, leave a 1" length, but if you are working longer stitches, leave a longer length.

In order for graph colors to contrast well, graph colors may not match yarn colors. For instance, a light yellow may be selected to represent the metallic cord color gold, or a light blue may represent white yarn.

When following a graph showing several colors, you may want to work all the stitches of one color at the same time. Some stitchers prefer to work with several colors at once by threading each on a separate needle and letting the yarn not being used hang on the wrong side of the work. Either way, remember that strands of yarn run across the wrong side of the work may show through the stitches from the front.

As you stitch, try to maintain an even tension on the yarn. Loose stitches will look uneven, and tight stitches will let the canvas show through. If your yarn twists as you work, you may want to let your needle and yarn hang and untwist occasionally.

When you end a section of stitching or finish a thread, weave the yarn through the back side of your last few stitches, then trim it off.

CONSTRUCTION & ASSEMBLY

After all pieces of an item needing assembly are stitched, you will find the order of assembly is listed in the Stitching Instructions and sometimes illustrated in Diagrams found with the graphs. For best results, join pieces in the order written. Refer to the Stitch Key and to the directives near the graphs for precise attachments.

FINISHING TIPS

To combat glue strings when using a hot glue gun, practice a swirling motion as you work. After placing the drop of glue on your work, lift the gun slightly and swirl to break the stream of glue, as if you were making an ice cream cone. Have a cup of water handy when gluing. For those times that you'll need to touch the glue, first dip your finger into the water just enough to dampen it. This will minimize the glue sticking to your finger, and it will cool and set the glue more quickly.

To attach beads, use a bit more glue to form a cup around the bead. If too much shows after drying, use a craft knife to trim off excess glue.

Scotchguard® or other fabric protectors may be used on your finished projects. However, avoid using a permanent marker if you plan to use a fabric protector, and be sure to remove all other markings before stitching. Fabric protectors can cause markings to bleed, staining yarn.

FOR MORE INFORMATION

Sometimes even the most experienced needlecrafters can find themselves having trouble following instructions. If you have difficulty completing your project, write to Plastic Canvas Editors, *The Needlecraft Shop*, 23 Old Pecan Road, Big Sandy, Texas 75755.

For supplies, first shop your local craft and needlework stores. If you are unable to find the supplies you need, write to the address below for a free catalog. The Needlecraft Shop *carries plastic canvas in a variety of shapes, sizes and colors, plastic canvas yarn and a large selection of pattern books.*

23 Old Pecan Road, Big Sandy, Texas 75755 (903) 636-4000 or (800) 259-4000

Stitch Guide

NEEDLEPOINT STITCHES

LONG STITCH
is a horizontal or vertical stitch used to stitch designs or fill in background areas. Can be stitched over two or more bars.

| 8 | 6 | 4 | 2 |
| 7 | 5 | 3 | 1 |

CONTINENTAL STITCH
can be used to stitch designs or fill in background areas.

	7	9
8	6	4	2
5	3	1

REVERSE CONTINENTAL STITCH
can be used to stitch designs or fill in background areas.

| 2 | 4 | 6 |
| 1 | 3 | 5 |

WHIPSTITCH
is used to join two or more pieces together.

SLANTED GOBELIN STITCH
can be used to stitch designs or fill in background areas. Can be stitched over two or more bars in vertical or horizontal rows.

	6
	4
5	2
3	1

OVERCAST
is used to finish edges. Stitch two or three times in corners for complete coverage.

HERRINGBONE WHIPSTITCH

	9		12
11		10
7		8
	1		6
		4
3		2

RYA KNOT
is used to fill in background areas or as an embroidery stitch to add a loopy or fringed texture. Stitch over two bars leaving a loop, then stitch over adjacent bars to anchor the loop.

| 1 | 25 | 6 |
| | 34 | 7 |

SCOTCH STITCH

	2	4	6	8
1				10
3			
5		
7	9	

MOSAIC STITCH

	6	4
5		2
3	1

CROSS STITCH
can be used as a needlepoint stitch or as an embroidery stitch stitched over background stitches with contrasting yarn or floss.

| 1 | 3 |
| | 2 |

SMYRNA CROSS STITCH
can be used as a needlepoint stitch or as an embroidery stitch stitched over background stitches with contrasting yarn or floss.

4	8	2
5		6
1	7	3

ALTERNATING SLANTED GOBELIN

| | 4 | 2 |
| 3 | 1 |

EMBROIDERY STITCHES

STRAIGHT STITCH
is usually used as an embroidery stitch to add detail. Stitches can be any length and can go in any direction. Looks like Backstitch except stitches do not touch.

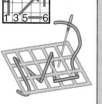

| 2 | | 4 |
| 1 | 3 | 5 | 6 |

FRENCH KNOT
is usually used as an embroidery stitch to add detail. Can be made in one hole or over a bar. If dot on graph is in hole as shown, come up and go down with needle in same hole.

| 1 | 2 |

BACKSTITCH
is usually used as an embroidery stitch to outline or add detail. Stitches can be any length and go in any direction.

| 5 | 6 | 1 | 2 |
| | 3 | 4 |

Acknowledgments

We would like to express our appreciation to the many people who helped create this book.
ır special thanks go to each of the talented designers who contributed original designs.
We also wish to express our gratitude to the following manufacturers for their generous contribution
materials and supplies for some of the featured projects:

Ad-Tech™
afty Magic Melt Glue: Lacy Coverlet, Roses are Red,
arbright Angel

Aleene's™
hick Designer Tacky Glue: The Nativity, Poinsettia Doorstop,
Celestial Christmas Orb

The Beadery®
bochons: Fancy Farm Animals

Bel-Tree Corporation
imal eyes: Cat Candy Wizard

ggle eyes: Scary-Crow

Bernat®
ındicrafter® Cotton Plastic Canvas Yarn: Loons Study Set

Crafter's Choice®
agnetic strips: Fancy Farm Animals

Darice®
ınvas: Loons Study Set, Forget-me-not Bureau Scarf, Lacy
verlet, House Blessing, Garden Delight, Roses are Red,
ight Sails Trio, Fancy Farm Animals, Mosaic Santa Bag,
askets of Violets, Garden Angel, Be Mine Monkey, Valentine
reath, Halloween Faces, Cat Candy Wizard, Scary-Crow

lon Plus™ yarn: Winter Jewels, Daily Inspirations, Patriotic
cnic Set, Cat Candy Wizard, Autumn Breezes, Southwestern
indows, Starbright Angel

etallic cord: Winter Jewels, Daily Inspirations, Lacy Coverlet,
oses are Red, Patriotic Picnic Set, Valentine Wreath, Cat
andy Wizard, Celestial Christmas Orb, Starbright Angel

ıffia straw: Poinsettia Doorstop, Celestial Christmas Orb

Delta
ramcoat® acrylic paint: The Nativity

DMC®
ımbroidery floss: Garden Delight, Southwestern Windows

pearl cotton: Summer Wind Jinglers, Baskets of Violets,
ıuthwestern Windows

Fibre Craft®
ectronic music box with lights: Musical Lights

J.&P. Coats / Coats & Clark / Anchor
Embroidery floss: Garden Angel

Pearl cotton: The Nativity

Plastic canvas yarn: Garden Angel

Kreinik
Metallic braid and metallic ribbon: Shimmering Bath Ensemble,
The Nativity, Halloween Faces

Kunin/Foss Manufacturing
Presto-Felt™: The Nativity

Rainbow Hair: Garden Angel

Mangelsen's®
Porcelain nativity doll parts: The Nativity

Mill Hill Beads from Gay Bowles Sales, Inc.
Bugle beads: Southwestern Windows

One & Only Creations®
Curly doll hair: Starbright Angel

Spinrite®
Plastic canvas yarn: Fancy Farm Animals

Streamline
Buttons: Scary-Crow

Uniek® Crafts
Canvas: Shimmering Bath Ensemble, Daily Inspirations, The
Nativity, Summer Wind Jinglers, Batter Up!, Celestial Christmas
Orb

Needloft® yarn: Topiary Tree, Forget-me-not Bureau Scarf, Lacy
Coverlet, House Blessing, Guardian Angel, Roses are Red,
Spiraling Star, Batter Up!, Mosaic Santa Bag, My Little Wagon,
Country Flag Sampler, Baskets of Violets, Halloween Faces,
Autumn Breezes, Scary-Crow, Southwestern Windows,
Poinsettia Card Caddy, Musical Lights, Starbright Angel

Metallic cord: Spiraling Star

Stuffing pellets: Poinsettia Doorstop

Wright's®
Lace trim: Starbright Angel

A special thanks to hand model Sandy Fults and to Craig & Jan Jaynes
and Kelly & Vinita Barfield for the use of their props.

Index

Designers